CRIMINAL JURISDICTION ALLOCATION IN INDIAN COUNTRY

Ronald B. Flowers

ASSOCIATED FACULTY PRESS, INC.
Port Washington, N.Y. // 1983

Associated Faculty Press, Inc.

Multi-disciplinary Studies in Law and Jurisprudence

Advisory Editor

Honorable Rudolph J. Gerber

Manufactured in the United States of America

Published by
Associated Faculty Press, Inc.
Port Washington, N.Y.

Library of Congress Cataloging in Publication Data

Flowers, Ronald B.
    Criminal jurisdiction allocation in Indian country.

    (Multidisciplinary studies in law and jurisprudence)
    Bibliography: p.
    Includes index.
    1. Indians of North America—Legal status, law, etc. 2. Criminal law—United States. I. Title. II. Series.
KF8210.C7F56 1983   345.73'01   83-6424
ISBN 0-8046-9324-2   347.3051

Preface

"Criminal Jurisdiction Allocation In Indian Country" seeks to explore the nature and distribution of authority between the Federal, State, and tribal governments concerning criminal conduct on Indian land. The book examines the Constitutional provisions with regard to this allocation, the historical foundations, and the resultant, often overlapping, sometimes confusing adjudication and governing of such land.

The book is a compilation of legislation and case law applicable to criminal jurisdiction in Indian Country, the U.S. Constitutional provisions regulating such authority, historical contributions to the current jurisdictional scheme, and the defining of what constitutes an "Indian" and "Indian land" as it pertains to such jurisdiction.

The major focus and importance of the research is to create a greater understanding of the basis and context of governmental authority over Indian land by which criminal jurisdiction is allocated between the Federal, State, and tribal governments and dispensed by their courts. The book is unique in that it investigates and is devoted entirely to a division of Federal law and the criminal justice system largely ignored – the governing scheme over criminal activity occurring on Federal Indian Territory in the United States. To help illustrate this are a number of significant court cases as they apply to the development of criminal jurisdiction in Indian Country.

The book will prove beneficial to libraries, Indian Services and Agencies, Indian historians, law students, criminal justice and ethnic study practitioners, and both Native Americans and non-Indians alike interested in U.S. Government-Indian relations, from its inception to the present, and how it relates to the allocation of jurisdictional authority involving criminal concerns between the representative governments.

Scholars will find the book valuable in the learning and teaching of the diverse interpretations of the Constitution, case law, Indian history, the differences in branches of government, research methods, and the criminal justice system. However, by no means is the material limited to scholars. Indeed, it is as easily grasped and appreciated by the interested layman, undergraduate, graduate, and scholar alike, in that the reader is sure to come away knowing more on the subject matter than they did previously.

Ronald Barri Flowers
May 11, 1983
Citrus Heights, California

Contents

Part I

Part II

Part III

Part I

Introduction

Indians born in the United States have long had problems with the National Government. These problems concern such things as Indian sovereignty, Indian self-determination, and jurisdictional disputes. Because of circumstances of varying legal and historical importance, tribal Indians have been subject, throughout the history of the United States, to many treaty provisions and special laws enacted by Congress for their governance. This has led to many court cases to decide exactly where the Indian stood with regard to such things as independence, laws, etc. Since the beginning of our National Government, authority to enact federal legislation pertaining to Indians has been vested in the federal government, first by the United States Constitution.

In Indian country, the division of criminal jurisdiction between federal, state, and tribal governments has been very complex. With federal legislation being unclear and overlapping jurisdictional authority to the federal, state, and tribal governments, it has been difficult to determine who has jurisdiction over what tribe, race, or crime. Tribal law present before federal legislation has further added to the problem of jurisdiction. It is this area of the United States Government—Indian relations—that we will try to understand better. Before one can understand jurisdictional disputes within Indian country, the terms Indian and Indian country must first be defined. This will be discussed in the first chapter. Chapter 2 will examine the historical foundation for the United States Government and the relation to Indian affairs. Chapters 3 and 4 will examine the early legislation and treaties dealing with the Indians. Chapter 5 will study the federal recognition of sovereignty. Chapters 6 and 7 will examine the allocation of criminal jurisdiction in Indian country; in Chapter 8, civil jurisdiction in Indian country will be discussed. Chapter 9 will concentrate on Indian sovereignty and Chapter 10 will explain some of the problems in the Jurisdictional scheme and offer some solutions. Chapter 11 will address the issue of whether or not the Indians have been treated fairly.

Chapter 1
Identifying the Indian

Before one can begin to understand the Indian and criminal jurisdictional problems in Indian country, three questions must be answered: (1) Who is an Indian?; (2) What is Indian country?; and (3) What is an Indian title?

Definition of an Indian

For the purpose of criminal jurisdiction, an Indian is a person who has some ethnic connection and some degree of Indian blood. The definition of "Indian" varies according to the statutes, case laws, and administrative enactments that have formulated different definitions. Often, the definition of Indian appears in the individual constitution of legal codes of a tribe. In general, however, certain considerations are relevant in order to be considered an Indian. These include: an individual's residence, the particular law involved, a person's degree of Indian blood, tribal enrollment, and an individual's opinion as to his own status. In Title 25 of the United States Code and the Code of Federal Regulations, the definitions of Indians vary, depending on the topic. For example, one section dealing with the court of Indian offenses states specifically that, for enforcement of regulations in that section, "an Indian shall be deemed to be any person of Indian descent who is a member of any recognized Indian tribe now under Federal jurisdiction."[1]

Without having specific criteria, other than statutory words, the courts in earlier decisions took the position that the term "Indian" is descriptive of an individual who not only has Indian blood, but who is also regarded as an Indian by the community of Indians in which he lives. With this in mind, in *United States* v. *Rogers*,[2] the court held that a white man adopted into an Indian tribe did not, therefore, become an Indian within the meaning of the statute. Other courts have largely followed the example of this case in determining who could be considered an Indian.

For purposes of legislation on Federal criminal jurisdiction, a person of mixed blood living on a reservation and enrolled in a tribe is an Indian.[3] "It has been held[4] that an individual of less than one-half Indian blood enrolled in a tribe and recognized as an Indian by the tribe is an Indian within the Act of March 4, 1909,[5] extending federal jurisdiction to rape committed by one Indian against another within the limits of an Indian reservation."[6] In a similar case, *Sloan* v. *United States*,[7] it has been held in that mixed-bloods are recognized by the tribe as members and they may, therefore, properly receive allotments of land as Indians. In *Sully* v. *United States*,[8] where one-eighth bloods were involved, the court stated that the persons were "of sufficient Indian blood to substantially handicap them in the struggle for existence," and held that "they were Indians and were entitled to be enrolled as such."[9]

State and federal courts have often debated the question of who is an Indian. In *State* v. *Phelps*,[10] an Indian was defined as "a person with some degree of Indian blood who has not severed his tribal relationship and who claims to be an Indian."[11] Indians who have severed ties with their tribes are sometimes treated as non-Indians for the purpose of criminal jurisdiction: *People* v. *Carmen*.[12] Generally speaking, aside from statutory definitions, the federal government, in dealing with Indian affairs, commonly considers a person who is of Indian blood and a member of a tribe an Indian, regardless of the degree of Indian blood in him. "Thus, the Indian Law and Order Regulations approved by the Secretary of the Interior on November 27, 1935 contain the provision: For the purpose of the enforcement of the Regulations in this part, an Indian shall be deemed to be any person of Indian descent who is a member of any recognized Indian tribe now under federal jurisdiction."[13]

In determining whether or not a person is an Indian, it basically depends on who is interpreting this and for what purpose. To determine whether or not a person who has committed a crime on a reservation is an Indian produces many problems. For one, it depends on who has jurisdiction over the crime committed. Also, the offender has to cooperate in determining this. Many offenders are well aware of the limitations of the law and could, therefore, act accordingly, depending on what crime they commit. For example, someone apprehended after committing a crime may deny or claim Indian status depending on what could happen to him. The many definitions Indian are troubleshome for tribal governments because the technicalities in determining who is an Indian tend to hinder the tribe's ability to effectively govern its territory.

What is Indian Country?

Indian country, at any given time, must be viewed with regard to the existing body of federal and tribal law. Until 1817, Indian country was land within which the criminal laws of the United States had not been made applicable. This meant that any crimes within this country whether white against white, or by Indians, were not recognized in federal or state courts because Congress had not issued jurisdiction in those courts for that purpose.

In general, the term "Indian country" has been used in many senses. It is most usefully defined as country in which federal laws relating to Indians and tribal customs are laws that are generally applicable. The phrase "generally applicable" is used because federal law, relating to Indians and tribal law and custom, have a validity regardless of locality. The greater part, however, of the body of federal and Indian law and tribal law applies only to certain areas which have a peculiar relation to the Indians and are referred to generally as "Indian country."[14]

The power to define Indian country is exclusively in the hands of the federal government. This power is derived from three sources. "First, the Constitution gives the President[15] and Congress[16] power over Indian affairs. The Supreme Court has construed these Constitutional grants as giving broad authority to the federal government.[17] Secondly, the courts have described the federal government's relationship to the tribe as that of a guardian to a ward.[18] Third, federal authority is inherent in the federal government's ownership of Indian occupied lands."[19] Treaties were the initial way in which Indian country was determined by Congress. The first Congressional procedure for determining Indian country was with the Indian Intercourse Act of 1834, which will be discussed in Chapter 3.

As the Indian titles were extinguished, those lands east of the Mississippi would discontinue being Indian country. The change in designation of Indian land west of the Mississippi would require new legislation to fix new boundaries. This would have to be consistent with the policy of relocating the Indians in the West. Allotted lands were also to be included in the federal determination of Indian country. These changes in legislative policy led to the United States Supreme Court expanding the definition of Indian country between 1834 and 1948.

The General Allotment Act of 1887, known as the Dawes Act, provided for the division of tribal lands by allotment to individual Indians. The United States held the titles to such allotments in trust for twenty-five years to prevent alienation. This law was motivated by Indian rights organizations which were convinced that allotment and assimilation were the only answers to the Indian problem. The Dawes Act addressed itself to not only the issue of collective landholding, but also to equally important issues such as tribal organization and the legal status of individual Indians. The Dawes Act was enacted to allow the Indian to have stronger retention of allotted lands and tribal affiliation and at the same time be acculturized into American society. A case that had a significant role in the Dawes Act was the *Elk* v. *Wilkins*[20] decision. In this case, the plaintiff, an Indian who had separated from his tribe and resided among the white people of Omaha, Nebraska, was denied the right to register to vote by Wilkins, the local registrar, on the grounds that he was not a United States citizen. This decision was upheld by the Supreme Court. "The decision in Elk acutely embarrassed the proponents of severality legislation. Their argument that tribalism had to be destroyed in order to allow the individual Indian to assume his rightful place in white society seemed, in the light of the Supreme Court's decision, either false, hyporcitical, or both. If the Indian were to lose his tribal affiliation and to move into white society, he would be left in limbo."[21]

Allotted lands were recognized as a part of Indian country in 1914 in *United States* v. *Peliam,*[22] where the court "decided that allotments held in trust by the United States for Indian allottees were still of distinctively Indian character and would remain Indian country for the period of the trust."[23] This decision was further reinforced in 1921 in *United States* v. *Ramsey.*[24] In this case, the court held that restricted allotments are part of Indian country until these restrictions are removed.

In addition to allotted lands, the definition of Indian country was further expanded with Supreme Court decisions. Two important cases along this course were *Donnelly* v. *United States,*[25] and *United States* v. *Sandoval.*[26] "In *Donnelly* v. *United States,* the court held that any change in the definition of Indian country was acceptable, provided that Congress or the Executive could demonstrate some change of circumstances necessitating the revision. In the same year, 1913, the court in *United States* v. *Sandoval* extended the definition of Indian country to reach the non-reservation lands of the Santa Clara Pueblo in New Mexico. In so doing, the court relied upon the plenary power of Congress over Indians and reasoned that Congress had the power to decide what was Indian country."[27]

In 1938, in *United States* v. *McGowan,*[28] the court held that any lands purchased by the federal government and set apart exclusively for Indian use fall within the definition of Indian country. This standard meant that those lands that were designated by the government for Indian use would be called Indian country.

In 1948, Congress enacted a comprehensive federal definition of Indian country. This was part of an act to revise the entire United States Criminal Code. The aim of this definition was to attempt to clarify the confusion that existed in the application of criminal laws to Indian country. This definition is current and it adopted the guidelines expressed in such cases as Sandoval, Gunnelly, Pelican, Ramsey, and McGowan. When enacting Title 18 of the United States Code, entitled "Crimes and Criminal Procedure," into law, Congress established the following definition of Indian country. "Except as otherwise provided in Sections 1154 and 1156 of this title, the term 'Indian country' means (a) all land within the limits of any Indian reservation under the jurisdiction of the United States Government, notwithstanding the issuance of any patent, and including right-of-way running through the reservation, (b) all dependent Indian communities within the borders of the United States whether within the original or subsequently acquired territory hereof, and whether within or without the limits of a state, and (c) all Indian allotments, the Indian titles to which have not been extinguished, including right-of-way running through the same."[29]

There are many ways of defining Indian country. Some of the court decisions mentioned illustrate these ways. However, the difficulty in applying these definitions in day-to-day situations has caused many problems in Indian law today. Problems often arise in such areas as fragmental land ownership where allotted Indian land overlaps with non-Indian land. This could cause land ownership disputes that could result in crime and violence. In these areas, criminal jurisdiction changes as often as land title changes. Criminal jurisdiction depends on whether the land is Indian owned or non-Indian owned as well as whether the individual is Indian or non-Indian. This makes it especially tough on law enforcement officers in dealing with these fragmented land ownerships that involve Indian land, because they often find it necessary to search tract books to determine whether criminal jurisdiction is within the state, federal, or tribal government.

Indian Title

The term "Indian title" implies Indian ownership or the right to land just because they had original possession of it. Whether or not this right is legitimate is a totally different research, morally and otherwise. In terms of the United States, Indian title has been used to distinguish aboriginal usage without definite recognition of this right by the United States from a recognized right of occupancy. As the United States assumed a sovereign position, they maintained the right and authority to honor or extinguish Indian title. The United States Government used this sovereign position to give them the right to extinguish Indian title and to control individual non-Indian dealings with the Indians. "*Johnson* v. *McIntosh*,[30] decided in 1823, rationalization to the appropriation of Indian land by the white man's government, the extinguishment of Indian title by that sovereignty has proceeded as a political matter, without any admitted legal responsibility in the sovereign to compensate the Indian for his loss. Exclusive title to the lands passed to the white discoverers, subject to the Indian title with power in the white sovereign above to extinguish that right by purchase or conquest."[31] In these terms, Indian title is merely a title given to land occupied by Indians by the sovereign (United States) that can be taken away at any time.

This type of Indian title has been referred to as being "sacred as the fee simple of the whites" as in the case of *Mitchel* v. *United States*.[32] It has never been held to constitute a title in fee simple in the absence of some type of official recognition by the United States Government. There is no Congressional recognition of an Indian's right to permanent occupancy of any particular land; there has to be definite intention by Congressional action to accord legal rights, not simply permissive occupation. In the *Hynes* v. *Grimes Packing Company*[33] decision, the Supreme Court held that the Indian right of occupancy was not a compensable right in the absence of specific federal recognition.

In *Tee-Hit-Ton Indians* v. *United States*,[34] claims of these Indians were rejected by the Court of Claims on the same grounds of non-recognition. In this case, Mr. Justice Reed states, "We think it must be concluded that the recovery in the Tillamook Case[35] was based upon statutory direction to pay for the aboriginal title in the special jurisdictional act to equalize the Tillamooks with neighboring tribes, rather than upon holding that there had been a compensable taking under the Fifth Amendment. This leaves unimpaired the rule derived from *Johnson* v. *McIntosh* that the taking by the United States of unrecognized Indian title is not compensable under the Fifth Amendment.

"This is true, not because an Indian or an Indian tribe has no standing to sue or because the United States has not consented to be sued for the taking or original Indian title, but because Indian occupation of land without government recognition of ownership creates no rights against taking or extinction by the United States protected by the Fifth Amendment or any other principle of law."[36]

The terms "national domain," "Indian reservation," and "public lands" should be defined. It is generally recognized that "the national domain is the total area, land and water embraced in the boundaries of the United States including its possessions." An Indian reservation is simply a part of the public domain set aside by proper authority for use and occupation by a group of Indians. The United States holds the title, and the right of use and occupancy is in the Indians.[37] The term "public lands," found in various land laws, is said to be used generally "to describe such lands as are subject to sale or other disposition under general law and not to lands that have been reserved by treaty, act of Congress, or executive proclamation."[38]

Conclusion

In order to be able to establish exactly what an Indian is and how to differentiate them from other races, general definitions of Indians, Indian country, and Indian title have been examined in this chapter. From the historical context in which this material was presented, one should be able to see the shaping of United States-Indian relations. Chapter 2 will look at the actual historical basis that shaped United States-Indian relations.

Footnotes
Chapter 1

1. 25 C.F.R., Sec. 11.2 CA(c), 1974.
5. 35 Stat. 1088, 1151.
6. Federal Indian Law, U.S. Department of the Interior, United States Government Printing Office, Washington, 1958, p. 8.
8. *Ibid,* p. 10.
11. *Immigration, Alienage and Nationality,* "The Allocation of Criminal Jurisdiction and Indian Country—Federal, State, and Tribal Relationships," University of California, *Davis Law Review,* Vol. 8, 1975, p. 433.
13. Federal Indian Law, p. 12.
14. Federal Indian Law, p. 14.
15. United States Constitution, Art. II, Sec. 2, cl. 2.
16. United States Constitution, Art. I, Sec. 8, cl. 3.
19. *Immigration, Alienage and Nationality,* p. 436.
21. Rose, Lawrence. *American Indians and the Law,* Transaction Book, New Jersey, 1976, p. 20.
23. *Immigration, Alienage and Nationality,* p. 435.
27. *Ibid,* p. 434.
29. United States Code, Crime and Criminal Procedures, Act of June 25, 1948, 62 Stat. 684.
31. Federal Indian Law, p. 19.
36. *Ibid,* p. 21, 348 United States 272, 284-285 (1955).
37. 58 I.D. 331, 343.
38 Federal Indian Law, p. 20.

Cases

Chapter 1

2. *United States* v. *Rogers*, 45 U.S. 567 (1846).
3. *Famous Smith* v. *United States*, 151 U.S. 50 (1894).
4. *United States* v. *Gardner*, 189 Fed. 690 (1911).
7. *Sloan* v. *United States*, 118 Fed. 283 (1902).
8. *Sulley* v. *United States*, 195 Fed.113 (1912).
10. *State* v. *Phelps*, 93 Mont. 227, 19 p. 2d, 319 (1933).
12. *People* v. *Carmen*, 43 C. 2d, 342 (1954).
17. *United States* v. *Hilliday*, 70 U.S. 407, 417-418 (1866).
18. *Cherokee Nation* v. *Georgia*, 30 U.S. (1831).
19. *Johnson Graham's Lessee* v. *McIntosh*, 21 U. S. (1823).
20. *Elk* v. *Wilkins*, 112 U.S. 94 (1884).
22. *United States* v. *Pelican*, 232 U.S. 442 (1914).
24. *United States* v. *Ramsey*, 271 U.S. 467 (1921).
25. *Donnelly* v. *United States*, 228 U.S. 243, 256-257 (1913).
26. *United States* v. *Sandoval*, 231 U.S. 2f (1913).
28. *United States* v. *McGowan*, 302 U.S. 535 (1938).
30. *Johnson* v. *McIntosh*, 8 Wheat. 543 (1923).
32. *Mitchel* v. *United States*, 9 Pet. 711, 746 (1835).
33. *Hynes* v. *Grimes Packing Company*, 337 U.S. 86 (1949).
34. *Tee-Hit-Ton Indians* v. *United States*, 120 F. Supp. 202 (1954).
35. *United States* v. *Tillamooks*, 341 U.S. 48 (1951).
38. *Newhall* v. *Sanger*, 92 U.S. 761, 763 (1875).

Chapter 2
Territorial Jurisdiction Foundation

In defining the United States Government's earliest relation-ship to the Indians, the historical foundation of this relation should be examined. The Constitution, as the supreme law of the United States, provided the legislative and executive branches of the federal government with a broad authorization for the exercise of power over Indian affairs. "Acting under the Articles of Confederation and under the Constitution, the new government of the United States of America has cautiously defined its relationship to the Indian nations by treaties and by legislative enactments. The government still feared the Indian nations, on its borders, and it sought to establish relations which would minimize conflict with them. The treaties and laws of this period acknowledged in principle that Indian law was supreme in the Indian territories."[1] Unfortunately, though, the federal government could not prevent contact between its American citizens and the Indian nations. This contact, in part, had a significant affect in altering Indian legal systems.

The Articles of Confederation, in 1777, provided that "Congress shall also have the sold and exclusive right and power of regulating the trade and managing all affairs with the Indians, not members of any of the States, provided that the legislative right of any state within its own limits not be infringed or violated."[2] With this charter as its guide, the new nation made its first treaty with the Delaware Indian nation in 1778. Article

IV of the Delaware Treaty established a way in which each nation would handle criminal violations within its own borders by citizens from others, and provide for the extradition of criminal fugitives. During this time, other treaties stipulated that United States citizens, within Indian nation boundaries, were subject to the tribe's national law.

The Confederation Congress also controlled United States citizens dealing with Indians. The Northwest Ordinance of July 13, 1787, provided: "The utmost good faith shall always be observed toward the Indians, their land and property shall never be taken from them without their consent; but laws founded in justice and humanity shall from time to time be made, for preventing wrongs being done to them, and for preserving peace and friendship with them."[3] At this time, and throughout the history of Indian affairs, the intentions by the government of justice toward the Indians was steadily stated.

With this purpose in mind, Congress followed the pattern set by the Articles of Confederation. The Constitution contains little mention of Indians. However, of the few words in the Constitution concerning Indians, there is a provision in the Constitution which is really the basis of most of the Indian-United States relations—Article I, Section 8, clause 3, which provides that: "The Congress shall have the Power to regulate Commerce with foreign Nations, and among the several States, and with the Indian tribes."[4] It is the part of this clause with regard to Indians that will be examined.

Congress, from the very beginning, has exercised its commerce power over the Indians in a preemptive way. As one can note, "foreign nations, states, and Indian tribes" are separately delineated. With the Constitution giving the legislature broad powers over Indian affairs through Article I, Section 8, clause 3, John Marshall recognized this fact in one of the first important Indian cases, *Worcester* v. *Georgia.*[5]

In this case, Marshall stated that "The Constitution confers on Congress the powers of war and peace; of making treaties, and of regulating commerce. . . with the Indian tribes. These powers comprehend all that is required for the regulation of our intercourse with the Indians. Of the three Constitutional elements of this general power to regulate Indians, two—the treaty-making[6] and commerce powers—have had continuing importance to Indian law in their own right."[7]

Historically, the power of Congress to regulate commerce with Indian tribes has the entire nation for its field of action, not just Indian country. The extent of this power has been demonstrated in the Indian liquor laws, which represented one of the early examples of federal control. Present law leaves the issue of liquor up to the states and the Indian tribes.

"The Commerce Clause is the only grant of power in the Federal Constitution which mentions Indians. The Congressional power over commerce with the Indian tribes plus the treaty-making power is much broader than the power over commerce between states. So long as 'Indian tribes' exist as such, or until the Constitution is amended, Congress ostensibly will retain the plenary power granted or implied in Article I, Section 8, clause 3, of the Constitution, to regulate tribal activities and thereby the activities of individual members. So far, citizenship for the Indian has presented on insurmountable obstacle to continued regulation."[8]

In addition to Article I, Section 8, clause 3, there are a few other lesser provisions in the Constitution which refer to Indians or tribes. Article I, Section 2, clause 3 and the Fourteenth Amendment, which amended it, exclude Indians not taxed for the purpose of determining a state's representation in the House of Representatives. Article I, Section 2, clause 3, in addition, excluded Indians not taxed from a state's apportionment of direct taxes. Article II, Section 2, clause 2, gives the President, with the consent of the Senate, the power to make treaties. (This will be further discussed in Chapter 4.) The other provision is the Tenth Amendment,[9] which divides the powers into three groups: United States, the States, and the people. In reality, the Tenth Amendment does not actually provide for Indian tribes. There is no other provision in the Constitution that can be read as a source of tribal power. Therefore, this closes the tribe's Constitutional rights to entity status.

This conclusion is supported by the fact that there is little mention regarding Indian tribes or Indians in *The Federalist Papers. The Federalist Papers* was written by Alexander

Hamilton, James Madison, and John Jay. It is a major document contemporaneous with the Constitution in that it actually defends the Constitution; it explains the complexities of the Constitutional government. Alexander Hamilton looked at the Indians as savages and the natural enemies of the United States and saw a justification for a standing army under the Constitution.[10] Hamilton also viewed the Indian nations as a threat to the Union.[11] John Jay, though also basically against Indians, was a bit more thoughtful in his attitude. He stated that "not a single Indian war has yet been produced by aggressions of the present federal government, feeble as it is; but there are several instances of Indian hostilities having been provoked by the improper conduct of individual states, who, either unable or unwilling to restrain or punish offenses, have given occasion to the slaughter of many innocent inhabitants."[12] James Madison, in commenting on commerce power with the Indian tribes, observed that Article I, Section 8 (3) cured imperfection in the Articles of Confederation, which had limited federal power to Indians not within a state.[13]

In this great document dealing with the Constitution of the United States, these are the only references made regarding Indians. This validates the conclusion that neither the Constitution nor its draftsmen provided for the continuing existence of Indian tribes. Forty years after the Federalist Papers, in 1828, James Kent predicted the doom of all Indians: "Indians have generally, and with some very limited exceptions, been unable to share in the enjoyment, or to exist in the presence of civilization and, judging from their past history, the Indian of the Continent appear to be destined, at no very distant period of time, to disappear with those vast forests which once covered the country, and the existence of which seems essential to their own."[14] Although this did not happen, it probably generalized the feelings at that time of the people and, possibly, the government.

A case that exercises the commerce clause of the Constitution is *United States* v. *Forty-Three Gallons of Whiskey*.[15] In this case, the Supreme Court declared: "Under the Articles of Confederation, the United States had the power of regulating the trade and managing all affairs with the Indians not members of any of the states; provided that the legislative right of a state within its own limits be not infringed or violated. Of necessity, these limitations rendered the power of no practical value. This was seen by the convention which framed the Constitution, and Congress now has the exclusive and absolute power to regulate commerce with the Indian tribes—a power as broad and as free from restrictions as that to regulate commerce with foreign nations."[16]

Congress, in exercising its power to regulate commerce with Indian tribes, has been the major architect of American law and policy. The commerce clause was designed not only to prevent state legislation against the Indians, but to also protect the Indians from white people and vice versa. Prentice and Egan describe the historic purpose of the commerce clause in *The Commerce Clause of the Federal Constitution,* 1898: "The purpose with which this power was given to Congress was not merely to prevent burdensome, conflicting or discriminating state legislation, but to prevent fraud and injustice upon the frontier, to protect an uncivilized people from wrongs by unscrupulous whites, and to guard the white population from the danger of savage outbreaks."[17] Congress has been inconsistent in regulating commerce with the Indians. It reflects the values and interests of the American society, henceforth, the Congressional treatment of Indians has fluctuated from total separation to total assimilation, and this has included the complete termination of tribal status.

Federal Sources of Power

The entire power of the United States Government over Indians and Indian tribes, discussed briefly in Chapter 1, emanates from three sources. The first was discussed in this chapter—the Constitution grants to Congress[18] and to the Presidents[19] powers over Indian affairs which has been interpreted as giving broad authority to the federal government.[20]

The second source of federal power is the court applied theory of guardian-ward relationship to the federal government's with the tribe.[21] "The courts, in maintaining that the liquor prohibition applied to Indians not residing on a reservation, recognized a second source of Congressional power—that implicit in the guardianship of the United States over the Indian[22]—which operated in conjunction with the Constitutional authority of the commerce clause.[23] The "guardian-ward theory" of Federal-Indian relations arose out of a direction in Chief Justice Marshall's opinion in *Cherokee Nation* v. *Georgia*,[24] and the federal judiciary has often relied upon it as a justification for the exercise of federal power as against both the states[25] and the tribe.[26]"[27] This theory is based on the weakness and dependency of the tribes on the federal government. It also emphasizes the government's obligation to aid the Indian in adjusting to an alien culture that has altered the Indian's traditional lifestyle. This guardianship theory has been responsible for: alienating his land;[28] excluding a tribal Indian from a state adultery law;[29] establishing a body of criminal law that can be applied to Indian country;[30] maintaining exclusive jurisdiction over crimes between Indians in Indian country;[31] and for establishing additional reasoning for the liquor prohibition.[32] (This will be discussed in more detail in Part II.)

Federal ownership is the third source of the plenary power of the United States, as discussed somewhat in Chapter 1 under Indian country and Indian title. "The doctrine of federal ownership originated in Johnson and Graham's *Lessee* v. *McIntosh*[33] where Marshall, in holding invalid a land patent granted by the Cherokee Nation, maintained that title was in the United States and was derived from the right of discovery exercised by the colonial forerunners of the new nation. According to Marshall, the Indian tribes held only an exclusive right of occupancy."[34] Like a landlord drawing up rules for his tenants, the federal government, as owner of the land on which Indians live, has declared what laws shall and shall not apply to its tenants on the reservation. "The basis of this unique landlord and tenant theory was restated in *United States* v. *Kagama*,[35] when the Supreme Court, in holding that the government's exclusive jurisdiction over the commission of major crimes by Indians on the reservation was not an unconstitutional interference with state authority, maintained that the power of the United States over Indian country and other 'federal enclaves' emanated from ownership of the country in which the Territories are, and the right to exclusive sovereignty which must exist in the National Government and can exist nowhere else."[36]

The sources of federal power, guardianship and ownership, tend to operate together. "Where a controversy taking place in Indian country does not involve Indians or Indian interests, as in a crime involving non-Indians on the resevrvation, the federal judiciary has tended to assume that exclusive federal jurisdiction over the crime does not exist even though the crime is committed on federally owned land.[37] Apparently, the federal landlord will deal exclusively with the persons and property its Indian tenants, but it does not feel it necessary to deal with controversies that, although arising on federal property, concern only non-Indians."[38]

Conclusion

This chapter has studied the Constitutional foundation of the United States Government-Indian relations. Article I, Section 8, clause 3 was the only real Constitutional basis for relations, although there were a few other Constitutional references to Indian tribes. The lack of Constitutional provisions for Indians in the Constitution verified that its framers had not really thought of or recognized Indians in relation to the shaping of the Country and establishment of the government. The power of the United States Government over Indians and Indian affairs is derived from three sources: the Constitution, federal guardianship, and federal ownership. It is here that the shaping of United States-Indian relationships get to be more understanding. The federal government owns the land which Indians occupy and also acts as protectors of those Indians. Indian country and Indian title are the government's controlling interests in the Indians with regard to jurisdiction, therefore, major problems that may arise with Indians, are clearly in the hands of the federal government. Chapter 3 will examine some of the early legislation with respect to the commerce clause of the Constitution and its effect on United States-Indian relations.

The United States Government used Article I, Section 8, clause 3 as the force or justification behind their decisions and interactions relating to Indian affairs. The government took advantage of this clause as its early legislation was specifically designed to limit state, county, and individual intrusion on Indian interests. The commerce clause itself did not specifically outline United States power over Indians or define its relationship to Indians. However, since there was virtually no mention of Indians in the Constitution, the commerce clause had to be expanded to fit the government's need.

Footnotes

Chapter 2

1. *American Criminal Law Review.* "In Our Image. . . ,After Our Likeness: The Drive for the Assimilation of Indian Court Systems," by Kirk Kickingbird, Spring, 76, Vol. 13, No. 1, p. 683.

2. *Articles of Confederation,* Art. IX, Sec. 4.

3. Kickingbird, p. 684.

4. Martone, Federick J. "American Indian Tribal Self-Government in the Federal System: Inherent Right or Congressional License?" *Notre Dame Lawyer,* Ap. 76, Vol. 51, No. 4, p. 603.

6. *United States Constitution,* Art. II, Sec. 2, cl. 2.

7. Prince, Monroe E., *Law and the American Indian.* (The Bobbs-Merrill Company, Inc., New York), 1973, p. 17.

8. *Federal Indian Law,* United States Department of the Interior, United States Government Printing Office, Washington: 1958, p. 27.

9. Martone, P. 603; *United States Constitution,* Tenth Amendment.

10. *The Federalist Papers,* by Alexander Hamilton, James Madison, and John Jay, 1788, New American Library, 1961, No. 24, p. 161.

11. *The Federalist,* No. 25, p. 163.

12. *The Federalist,* No. 4, p. 44.

13. *The Federalist,* No. 42, p. 268-269.

14. Martone, p. 604.

16. *Federal Indian Law,* p. 27.

17. *Ibid,* p. 28.

18. *United States Constitution,* Art. I, Sec. 8, cl. 3.

19. *United States Constitution,* Art. II, Sec. 2, cl. 2.

27. Prince, p. 19.

34. *Ibid,* p. 21.

36. 118 United States at 380, Prince, p. 20.

38. Prince, p. 22.

Cases

Chapter 2

5.   *Worcester* v. *Georgia*, 31 U.S. (6 Pet.) 515 (1832).
15.   *United States* v. *Forty-Three Gallons of Whiskey*, 93 U.S. 188, 194 (1876).
20.   *United States* v. *Hilliday*, 70 U.S. 407, 417–418 (1866).
21.   *Cherokee Nation* v. *Georgia*, 30 U.S. 1, 9 (5 Pet.), 1, 12 (1831) *United States* v. *Nice*, 241 U.S. 591, 597-98 (1916).
22.   *United States* v. *Hilliday*, 70 U.S. 407, 417–418 (1866).
23.   *United States* v. *Hilliday*, 70 U.S. 407, 417–418 (1866).
24.   30 U.S. 1, 9 (5 Pet.) 1, 12 (1831): "(The Indians) are in a state of pupilage; their relation to the United States resembles that of a ward to his guardian."
25.   *United States* v. *Kagama*, 118 U.S. 375, 383 (1886).
26.   *United States* v. *Clapox*, 35 F. 575, 577 (D. Ore. 1888).
28.   *Tiger* v. *Wester Investment Co.*, 211 U.S. 286 (1911).
29.   *State* v. *Campbell*, 53 Minn. 354, 55 N.W. 553 (1893).
30.   *United States* v. *Kagama*, 118 U.S. 375, 383 (1886).
31.   *United States* v. *Pelican*, 232 U.S. 442, 447 (1914).
32.   *Hallowell* v. *United States*, 221 U.S. 317, 324 (1911).
33.   *Johnson and Graham's Lessee* v. *McIntosh*, 21 U.S. (1823).
35.   *United States* v. *Kagama*, 118 U.S. 375, 383, (1886).
37.   *Langford* v. *Monteith*, 102 U.S. 145 (1880); *Draper* v. *United States*, 164 U.S. 240 (1896).

Chapter 3
The Formative Era

In Chapter 2, it was determined that federal policy was geared toward protection of the Indians and control of state and individual dealings with the Indians; this was established with the commerce clause in the United States Constitution. The extent of tribal self-government, the entity status of the tribe, and tribal immunity from state interference are not guaranteed anywhere in the United States Constitution. These matters have historically been under the legislative power of Congress under the commerce clause, Article I, Section 8(3). Accordingly, law and policy have been dictated by the times.

In examining the early legislation toward the Indians, the years between 1790–1834 is known as the formative era. In less than a year after the Constitution was ratified, Congress enacted its first measure in governing relations between Indian tribes and citizens of the United States. It was the first of a series of non-intercourse acts to be adopted during the next 44 years. This first act was the Act of July 22, 1790.[1] This measure, which attempted to protect Indians, vested federal courts with jurisdiction over crimes committed by citizens against the property or person of peaceful or friendly Indians. The 1790 law was renewed by the Act of March 1, 1793.[2] President Washington remarked on this by stating, "A rigorous execution of justice on the violators of peace. . .is most likely to conciliate their [Indian's] attachment [to the United States]."[3] These acts were designed to keep Americans away from Indians. For example, a federal license was required to trade with tribes. These acts also prohibited the alienation of Indian land to Americans or to any of the states, without a federal treaty authorizing it. The third non-intercourse act was more elaborate than the first two. It set boundaries between Indian country and the rest of the United States territory. This act also established the death penalty for the non-Indian's murder of an Indian on tribal land. After expiring on its own, this act was replaced by a fourth act,[4] which expired on March 3, 1802. This act was not replaced until March 3, 1813.[5] Between 1802 and 1813, there existed no federal legislation to regulate affairs with Indians. The objective of these non-intercourse acts was to guarantee westward settlement and, at the same time, minimize conflicts between Indians and non-Indians.

"After 44 years of experience with sporadic non-intercourse acts, the first major piece of federal Indian legislation emerged, the Intercourse Act of 1834.[6] The frontier was advancing at an even faster rate, and the time had come to establish a more permanent mechanism by which non-Indian conflicts with Indians could be minimized. It provided licensing for trade with Indians,[7] prohibited non-Indians from bartering with Indians for hunting and cooking items,[8] prohibited non-Indians from hunting in Indian country,[9] prohibited non-Indian from grazing their animals in Indian country,[10] prohibited settlement on Indian land,[11] prohibited the conveyance of Indian land except by federal treaty,[12] prohibited speeches in or messages to Indian country designed to disturb the peace,[13] and extended federal criminal jurisdiction to all crimes committed in Indian country, except as 'to crimes committed by one Indian against the person or properties of another Indian."[14]

Conclusion

This chapter has examined the major historical pieces of legislation toward Indian affairs enacted by Congress under its power to regulate commerce. The major emphasis in this era, between 1790 and 1834, was to control non-Indian and state interaction with the Indians. This was accomplished through a series of non-intercourse regulations defining what non-Indians could and could not do concerning Indians and under what conditions they could do things. The purpose of this early legislation was to promote western expansion and to curb Indian hostilities. Chapter 4 will examine some of the early treaty approaches to jurisdiction of Indian country.

The power to make treaties was concurrent with the commerce clause. Article II, Section 2, gave the President and Congress the power to make treaties. This power extended from the commerce power to regulate trade with the Indians. The treaty-making efforts of the United States never operated as smoothly as the federal government had perhaps intended. There were many treaties that were rushed and illegal, and there were disagreements between non-Indians over land rights, some treaties were overlapped, terms of the treaties were not honored, and time limits expired, all making many treaties obsolete. In short, the treaty-making process was never smoothly handled and some of the problems associated with treaties, such as territorial disputes and land rights, can still be felt today. The treaty years lasted from the early 1700s to 1868.

Footnotes

Chapter 3

1. Act of July 22, 1790, Ch. 33, Sec. 5, 1 Stat. 137, 138.

2. Act of March 1, 1793, Ch. 19, Sec. 4, 1 Stat. 329.

3. Kickingbird, Kirk. "In Our Image. . .After Our Likeness: The Drive For the Assimilation of Indian Court Systems," *American Criminal Law Review,* Sp. 76, Vol. 13, No. 4, p. 684.

4. Act of March 3, 1799, Ch. 46, 1 Stat. 743.

5. Act of March 3, 1813, Ch. 61, 2 Stat. 829. This Act allowed the President to retaliate against the British for those injuries done to Americans by Indians aligned with the British in the War of 1812.

6. Act of June 30, 1834, Ch. 161, 4 Stat. 729 (codified in different sections of 25 U.S.C.).

7. Id. Sec. 2.

8. Id. Sec. 7.

9. Id. Sec. 8.

10. Id. Sec. 9.

11. Id. Sec. 11.

12. Id. Sec. 12.

13. Id. Sec. 13.

14. Martone, Federick J. "American Indian Tribal Self-Government in the Federal System: Inherent Right or Congressional License?", *Notre Dame Lawyer,* Vol. 51, No. 4, Ap. 76, Id. Sec. 13, p. 609.

Chapter 4
History of Government/Indian Treaties

Chapter 4 will examine, in brief, the historical process of treaties between the United States and Indians and its effect on United States-Indian policy. The original thirteen colonies entered into many treaties with Indian tribes.[1] As noted in Chapter 1, the initial United States-Indian relations and deals were made strictly by treaty. The colonial reservations were the precursors of the later federal reservations. By 1700, most of the Massachusetts Indians were placed on colonial reservations.[2] At the time, though, the colonists expected the assimilation of Indians into Massachusetts society, and so the reservation system was not meant to be permanent.[3] By the time the United States started the federal reservation policy for the Indian tribes in 1786, the Massachusetts reservation system had already served its purpose and had virtually ended.

When the colonies dealt with Indian tribes before they separated from Great Britain, they also dealt with Indian tribes through treaties during the Revolutionary War. The first federal treaty with a tribe was in 1778, with the Delaware Indians.[4] This was designed to keep these indians from aligning with the British during the war. The new United States guaranteed to the Delaware Indians any territory that they were entitled to by former treaties.[5]

The only Constitutional provision dealing with Indian treaties was Article II, Section 2(2), which gives the President and the

Senate the power to make treaties. This article required only Senate ratification. Therefore, the House of Representatives was never involved with Indian treaties. The Senate started off where the Continental Congress left off. Between the years 1778 and 1868, the last year in which the United States dealt with Indian tribes by treaty, the Senate ratified 370 Indian treaties.[6]

The use of treaties in dealing with the Indians in the formative era of American expansion was a natural phenomenon. It was preferred that westward expansion be accomplished by voluntary relinquishment of the territory, if possible, and if not, then by war. It was decided early that treaties entered into with Indian tribes required Senate ratification and had the same dignity and status as agreements with sovereign nations.

As U.S. power expanded, the use of treaties with Indians raised serious questions. These treaties suggested sovereignty in the tribe. What was thought to be necessary in the seventeenth and eighteenth centuries became somewhat of an embarrassment by the nineteenth century. As early as 1817, Andrew Jackson had written to President Monroe, "I have long viewed treaties with the Indians an absurdity not to be reconciled to the principles of our government. The Indians are the subjects of the United States, inhabiting its territory and acknowledging its sovereignty, then is it not absurd for the sovereign to negotiate by treaty with the subject?"[7] While the implication of tribal sovereignty arising from treaties may appear accurate, an examination of a typical treaty suggests the contrary. "In the treaty between the United States and the Cherokees in 1835,[8] the Cherokees ceded all their land east of the Mississippi River to the United States for $5 million.[9] The United States ceded lands west of the Mississippi River to the Cherokee tribe and agreed that the lands so ceded would never be included within the territorial limits of a state or territory without its consent.[10] The United States also promised that the tribe could make its own laws and be governed by them, 'provided always that they shall not be inconsistent with the Constitution of the United States and such acts of Congress as have been or may be passed regulating trade and intercourse with the Indians, and also, that they [Cherokee laws] shall not be considered as extending to such citizens and army of the United States as may travel or reside in Indian country by permission of the United States.' "[11] In other words, the tribe here was subjected to the sovereignty of the United States. For instance, the tribe was granted self-governing power, but subject to the Constitution and Congress and this power did not include non-Indians entering Indian country. The very terms of the treaty deny the tribe the sovereignty that they are supposed to have by virtue of that treaty.

Whatever inference was raised regarding tribal sovereignty by use of the treaty, power of the United States was soon to be no longer needed. By the Act of March 3, 1871.[12] the United States Congress proclaimed that: "[H]ereafter no Indian nation or tribe within the territory of the United States shall be acknowledged or recognized as an independent nation, tribe, or power with whom the United States may contract by treaty. . ."[13]

After this point, no treaty was made with an Indian tribe. There can be no clearer way to see how tribal sovereignty was extinguished. Existing treaties with Indian tribes have a status no greater than that of a statute and therefore can be repealed by an act of Congress.

Conclusion

In this chapter, it can be seen that treaties were the initial basis of United States-Indian transactions. The United States, at this time, accepted the treaties as official and recognizance of Indian country as sovereign. This was soon to change as the United States outgrew its need for treaties with the Indians as a result of expansion, power, and sovereignty itself.

However, when the treaties were in force they were used for just about every sort of transaction with the Indians including jurisdiction. Many of the treaties dealt with the difficult political problems created by criminal offenses of whites against Indians or Indians against whites.

Some of the earlier treaties adopted rules regarding both sides equal. Indians committing offenses against Federal or State laws outside the Indian country were subject to punishment by Federal or State courts. On the other side, whites committing offenses within Indian country against Indian laws were subjected to punishment by the Indian tribe.

Some treaties adopted an adjusted rule, similar to that found in treaties between the United States and various oriental countries.[14] The United States was granted jurisdiction over its citizens in Indian country, for appropriate punishment for any offense they might commit. The Indian tribe delivered such offenders to agents of the United States Government.[15] There were a number of treaties which gave the federal government authority to punish those Indians who committed offenses against non-Indians even if they occurred within Indian country.[16] After the treaty-making period ended, the federal government then asserted its jurisdiction over offenses committed by Indians against Indians within Indian country. Most treaties contained no express provisions on civil jurisdiction and so, in the absence of federal legislation, it was tribal law that governed the members of the tribe within the Indian country, to the exclusion of state law.

Chapter 5 will examine the friction that developed during territorial disputes between the United States and Indians in the treaty years. The legal status of Indian tribes in the United States and the important cases that set precedence in that respect will then be studied.

The treaty years were turbulent ones because Indian resistance was at its peak. Whether the treaties were legal or illegal, Indians did not want to give up their homeland and move westward to unknown territory. Many battles ensured between the Indians and non-Indians because of this. The Indians were eventually cast aside.

The Indian Removal Act of 1830 was Congress' legal aim at justifying the brutality and forceful eviction of thousands upon thousands of Indians. It forced the Indian to move westward against his own will. The land was bought from the Indians via treaties for sums far less than what the land was really worth. The U.S. Government could not control its own people—non-Indians, in many cases, simply took what they wanted or killed and maimed Indians just for pleasure.

The concept of sovereignty and the legality of relocation were tested in court in the 1830s with the Cherokee Nation challenging Georgia. The Cherokee Nation was affirmed to be sovereign in and of itself but it was still said to be a ward of United States and subject to its jurisdiction.

Footnotes

Chapter 4

1. See Indian Treaties 1736–1762 (Historical Society of Pennsylvania ed. 1938).

2. Kawashima, "Legal Origins of the Indian Reservation in Colonial Massachusetts", 13 AM. J. *Legal History* 42 (1969).

3. Id. at 56.

4. Treaty with the Delaware, Sept. 17, 1778, Stat. 13.

5. Id., Art. 6 at 14.

6. House Comm. of Interior and Insular Affairs, 88th Cong., 2d Sess., Lists of Indian Treaties 1–6 (Comm. Print. No. 33, 1964).

7. Higgins, "International Law Consideration of the American Indian Nations by the United States", 3 Ariz. L. Rev. 74, 82, (1961), quoting from Basset, Correspondence of Andred Jackson 279-281 (1955).

8. Treaty with the Cherokees, Dec. 29, 1835, 7 Stat. 478 (1835).

9. Id., Art. 1 at 479.

10. Id., Art. 5 at 481.

11. Martone, Frederick J. "American Indian Tribal Self-Government in The Federal System: Inherent Right or Congressional License", Notre Dame Lawyer, Vol. 51, No. 4, April 76, p. 606.

12. Y1 25 U.S.C., Sec. 71 (1970).

13. Martone, p. 607.

14. E.G., Art. 21 of Treaty of July 3, 1844, with China, 8 Stat. 529, 596.

15. E.G., Art. 6 of Treaty of August 24, 1818, Quapow Tribe, 7 Stat. 176, 177.

16. E.G., Art. 9 of Treaty of January 21, 1785, Wyandottes and Others, 7 Stat. 16, 17; Art. 6 of Treaty of November 28, 1785, Cherokee, 7 Stat. 18.

Chapter 5
Territorial Disputes and the Legal Status of Indians

On a superficial level, the early laws of the new struggling nation were sincere and were intended to maintain peaceful relations with the still-powerful Indian nations. The treaty-making process was meant to focus on this perspective of U.S.-Indian dealings. In reality, though, everything pointed to the fact that the Republic had every intention of obtaining as much land, as quickly as possible, from the Indians whether honestly or not. The stage for expansion had long been set: the treaties for land cessions, such as the Penn "walking treaty," the practice of genocide wherever and whenever the Indians were unwilling to part with their land.

Indian resistance continued not only against the new government, but also against individual pressures from non-Indians. Sometimes the struggles blossomed into Holy Wars. During the Pontiac rebellion, prior to the Revolutionary War, Lord Jeffrey Amherst, Commander of the British forces, introduced germ warfare when he ordered distribution of blankets infested with small pox to the Indian camps. This rebellion ended with another Indian defeat—an example of some of the cruelties used to remove Indians from their land.

The United States began early to intimidate Indian tribes into signing treaties which yielded huge areas of land. When intimidation failed, there was always an epidemic or the spreading of alcohol that, deliberate or otherwise, equally devastated tribal power and sometimes wiped out entire tribes. Around the beginning of the nineteenth century, American "Indian policy" started to evolve.

"President Thomas Jefferson first proposed the removal of Indians from the eastern states to a region west of the Mississippi where they might continue to live, undisturbed by civilization. The program had a few drawbacks. First, the frontier was moving West faster than would prove safe for the removed Indians. Second, the Indians to be sent West would lose land, resources, and improvements which the government had no right to deprive them of, by legislation. 'Removal' began to be debated in 1802 and later became a popular policy."[1]

In 1812, the Shawnee Tribe, similar to other midwestern tribes, was continually harassed and conned into ceding its land. The government appointed several Indians as chiefs of their tribes to represent the tribe in land cession treaties. In this same manner, the Sac and Fox tribes lost 50 million acres of land; the Delaware tribe lost three million acres, for which they were only offered $7,000. Many other tribes lost millions of acres in the same way. Sometimes the government did not even wait for treaties, but extinguished, by legislation, Indian title (see Chapter 1) to occupied lands. The Shawnee tribe, under Techumseh, rebelled against an illegal treaty and helped organize other tribes for similar rebellions. They also urged the British to help them. The Indian war was lost, even though the British had captured the nation's capitol, and Tecumseh was killed. The Creek Indian wars were similar to the Shawnee wars. It was during this conflict that Andrew Jackson introduced the scored earth method of warfare. In the treaty at Fort Jackson, at the end of the war, Jackson stripped the Creek nation of all remaining eastern land, thereby preparing them for removal.

When Andrew Jackson was elected President, the Indian removal policy was on its way to becoming law. In Jackson's first annual message on December 8, 1829, he set forth his program to move the Indians West of the Mississippi River. Speaking to the members of the Senate and the House of Representatives, Jackson delivered his message:

> The condition and ulterior destiny of the Indian tribes within the limits of some of our States have become

objects of much interest and importance. It has long been the policy of Government to introduce among them the arts of civilization, in the hope of gradually reclaiming them from a wondering life. This policy has, however, been coupled with another wholly incompatible with its success. Professing a desire to civilize and settle them, we have at the same time lost no opportunity to purchase their lands and thrust them farther into the wilderness. By this means they have not only been kept in a wandering state, but been led to look upon us as unjust and indifferent to their fate. Thus, though lavish in its expenditures upon the subject, Government has constantly defeated its own policy, and the Indians in general, receding farther and farther to the West, have retained their savage habits. A portion, however, of the Southern tribes, having mingled much with the whites and made some progress in the arts of civilized life, have lately attempted to erect an independent government within the limits of Georgia and Alabama. These States claiming to be the only sovereigns within their territories, extended their laws over the Indians, which induced the latter to call upon the United States for protection.

Under these circumstances the question presented was whether the General Government had a right to sustain those people in their pretensions. The Constitution declares that "no new State shall be formed or erected within the jurisdiction of any other State" without the consent of its legislature. If the General Government is not permitted to tolerate the erection of a confederate State within the territory of one of the members of this Union against her consent, much less could it allow a foreign and independent government to establish itself there. Georgia became a member of the Confederacy which eventuated in our Federal Union as a sovereign State, always asserting her claim to certain limits. . .Alabama was admitted into the Union on the same footing with the original States, with boundaries which were prescribed by Congress. There is no Constitutional, conventional, or legal provision which allows them less power over the Indians within their borders than is possessed by Maine or New York. . . .

Actuated by this view of the subject, I informed the Indians inhabiting parts of Georgia and Alabama that their attempt to establish an independent government would not be counteranced by the Executive of the United States, and advised them to emigrate beyond the Mississippi or submit to the laws of those States. . . .

A State cannot be dismembered by Congress or restricted in the exercise of her Constitutional power. But the people of those States and of every State, actuated by feelings of justice and a regard for our national honor, submit to you the interesting question whether something cannot be done, consistently with the rights of the States to preserve this much-injured race.

As a means of effecting this end I suggest for your consideration the propriety of setting apart an ample district West of the Mississippi, and without the limits of any State or Territory now formed, to be guaranteed to the Indian tribes as long as they shall occupy it, each tribe having a distinct control over the portion designated for its use. There they may be secured in the enjoyment of governments of their own choice, subject to no other control from the United States than such as may be necessary to preserve peace on the frontier and between the several tribes. There the benevolent may endeavor to teach them the arts of civilization and, by promoting union and harmony among them, to raise up an interesting commonwealth, destined to perpetuate the race and to attest the humanity and justice of this Government.

This emigration should be voluntary, for it would be as cruel and as unjust to compel the aborigines to abandon the graves of their fathers and seek a home in a distant land. But they should be distinctly informed that if they remain within the limits of the States they must be subject to their laws. In return for their obedience as individuals they will without doubt be protected in the enjoyment of those possessions which they have improved by their industry. . . .

The charter of the Bank of the United States expires in

1836, and its stockholders will most probably apply for a renewal of their privileges. In order to avoid the evils resulting from precipitancy in a measure involving such important principles and such deep pecuniary interests, I feel that I cannot, in justice to the parties interested, too soon present it to the deliberate consideration of the Legislature and the people. Both the Constitutionality and the expediency of the law creating this bank are well questioned by a large portion of our fellow citizens, and it must be admitted by all that it has failed in the great end of establishing a uniform and sound currency.

Under these circumstances, if such an institution is deemed essential to the fiscal operations of the Government, I submit to the wisdom of the Legislature whether a national one, founded upon the credit of the Government and its revenues, might not be devised which would avoid all Constitutional difficulties and at the same time secure all the advantages to the Government and country that were expected to result from the present bank. . . ."[2]

The message proved to be important because it recognized some of the problems between the States and the Indians and the plan to move the Indians westward. It also set forth conditional recognition of sovereignty for those tribes that cooperated.

Congress supported Jackson's program and the Indian Removal Act[3] became law in 1830. It provided for the exchanging of lands West of the Mississippi to which the United States claimed title, for those lands which the tribes held East of the Mississippi. The Indian Removal Act had its creation in the unstable political situation that was created by land-hungry settlers. In finding that it could not control its own citizens, the young, unstable United States Government began to fear that an Indian war would result from white encroachment on Indian territory.[4] The United States first thought to buy Indian land. However, when it became obvious that the Indians would not sell, Congress presented the idea of Indians exchanging their homeland for title to land in another part of the United States.[5]

The initial stages of Indian removal were quite hectic. Cherokees, Choctaws, Chicassaws, Creeks, and Seminoles were rounded up and herded like animals over the "Trail of Tears" to Oklahoma. More than 100 people died every day because of starvation, exhaustion, and brutality at the hands of the U.S. Army as well as American citizens. Even before Indians were out of eyesight of their property, it was being auctioned off to whites. Of the 50,000 Indians from the many tribes that were forced to leave their homes, approximately half of them died. Yet in President Van Buren's report to Congress on the progress of Indian removal in December of 1838, he announced: "It affords me sincere pleasure to apprise the Congress of the entire removal of the Cherokee Nation of Indians to their new homes West of the Mississippi. The measures authorized by Congress at its last session have had the happiest effects. By an agreement concluded with them by the commanding general in that country, their removal has been principally under the conduct of their own chiefs, and they have immigrated without any apparent reluctance."[6]

When they arrived in Oklahoma, those leaders of the Cherokee and Creek nations who signed the illegal treaties agreeing to removal were executed. These executions were under the authority of the "Blood Laws" of the nations, which forbid any treaties exchanging or selling their lands. After seven years of intra-tribal problems over the illegal treaties, the United States Government stepped in to mediate and to reimburse the tribes for the harsh suffering they had been through. However, the tribes had to pay for their own removal out of the small allowances held for them in the United States Treasury as payment for those lands stolen from them.

The only successful resistance of the removal was by the Seminole tribe. The Seminole war, waged by the United States Army, not only cost $50 million, but also resulted in the death of 1,500 men. Thousands of the Seminoles were finally removed; truce flags were ignored and many leaders were murdered.

"Eventually, approximately 80 tribes were forced to resettle in Oklahoma territory. Boundaries established for one tribe were moved to squeeze in additional tribes. 'Civilization' caught up to the removal lands before the tribes were resettled, but not before they had lost over 300 million acres of land to the speculators of the new democracy. All the tribal governments were outlawed to prepare for Oklahoma statehood. Thus, the farce was completed."[7]

The policy of Indian removal was heatedly debated in the national press and in the federal and state legislative bodies. As in the issue of slavery a few years earlier, the debates threatened to tear the Union apart. The state of Georgia led the proponents for removal and the Cherokee nation was quick to suffer the consequences of Georgia's position. "When gold was discovered on Cherokee lands in northern Georgia, the greedy reprobates who had immigrated to Georgia from the European prisons would recognize no law greater than their own. The state of Georgia outlawed the Cherokee nation's right to self-government and enforced their rulings by using vigilante groups. They killed and raped, and burned Indian farms and property, arresting and driving out sympathetic whites."[8] The Cherokee tribes, however, were unwilling to leave their traditional homes. The friction between the tribes and the whites over the control of territories increased. The conflict was soon brought before the Supreme Court in two famous cases, which not only addressed the legal status of Indian tribes in the United States, but also addressed the allocation of legal jurisdiction among the Indian, state, and federal courts.

The first case was *Cherokee Nation* v. *Georgia.*[9] In this case, the state of Georgia laid claim to those lands within the Cherokee national boundaries and went on to pass laws purporting to affect those lands. The Georgia law challenged not only those laws passed by the Cherokee National Council, but also the very existence of the Cherokee Nation. The Cherokee Nation brought suit in the United States Supreme Court invoking its original jurisdiction under the commerce clause in Article III of the United States Constitution because the controversy involved a dispute between a state and a foreign nation, the Cherokee Nation. Chief Justice Marshall avoided the issue of state or federal supremacy by declaring the Cherokee not to be a foreign nation:

> Though the Indians are acknowledged to have an unquestionable and heretofore, unquestioned right to the lands they occupy until that right shall be extinguished by

a voluntary cession to our government; yet it may well be doubted whether the tribes which reside within the acknowledged boundaries of the United States can, with strict accuracy, be denominated domestic dependent nations. They occupy a territory to which we assert a title independent of their will, which must take effect in point of possession when their right of possession ceases. . . . Meanwhile, they are in a state of pupilage. The relation to the United States resembles that of a ward to his guardian. . . . At the time the Constitution was formed, the ideas of appealing to an American court of justice for an assertion of right of redress of wrong, had perhaps never entered the mind of an Indian or his tribe.[10]

The significance of the *Cherokee Nation* v. *Georgia* decision lies in Chief Justice Marshall's choice of words. Phrases such as "domestic dependent nation" and "A ward to his guardian" did pretty much spearhead the U.S. Government's role of its relation to the Indian tribes. The concept of the United States as the guardian to its wards—the Indian tribe—is the basis for the federal government's role in Indian affairs, even today.

Another important case of tribal sovereignty, went to the Supreme Court a year later. In this issue, a missionary, Samuel Worcester, was arrested and prosecuted by the state of Georgia for entering Cherokee land in violation of Georgia law, but in conformity with Cherokee law. "In *Worcester* v. *Georgia*,[11] the court declared that the Indian nations '. . .had always been considered as distinct, independend political communities, retaining their own natural rights. . . .'[12] Writing for the majority, Chief Justice Marshall did not refer to the Indians' dependent status which he had announced in the earlier Cherokee case. On the contrary, he affirmed the sovereignty of the Cherokee Nation when he said, 'The settled doctrine of the law of the nation is, that a weaker power does not surrender its independence—its right to self-government—by association with a stranger, and taking its protection.'[13] In this decision the court rejected the idea that state laws can have any effect on Indians within tribal boundaries: 'The Cherokee Nation, then, is a distinct community, occupying its own territory, with boundaries accurately described, in which the laws of

Georgia can have no force and which the citizens of Georgia have no right to enter, but the assent of the Cherokees themselves, or in conformity with treaties, and with the acts of Congress.'[14] The tribes had little trouble in maintaining internal order until whiteman influence began to break up tribal values and customes. Some Indian commissioners reported that the per capita annuity payments were lessing the power of the tribal governments to maintain law and order."[15]

" 'Commissioners of Indian Affairs recognized the strength of Indian institutions: though it appeared to be the casual white observer that anarchy reigned in Indian encampments, those societies had evolved their own patterns of law and order. While they lacked law in the sense of formal written codes, of course, there were defined customary codes of behavior enforced by public opinion and religious sanction.'[16] The Commissioners, however, did not use traditional Indian institutions to solve Indian problems. On the contrary, they sought solutions for the white culture. An example of this was in 1833 and 1838 when the Commissioner of Indian Affairs recommended that a general written code be established for use by the tribes. Instead of using the law to control its own citizens, the United States increased military personnel near Indian reservations to keep unscrupulous whites away from the Indians."[17]

When the Indians turned to the federal government for justice more often than not they ran into prejudical attitudes. It was extraordinary for the murderer of an Indian to be convicted in New England. It was equally not unusual for horse thieves in Montana to be captured by federal troops with Indian stock in their possession and then be freed by a federal grand jury. The courts manifested their prejudice not only in unequal protection of Indians, but also through judicial decisions which sharply curtailed the jurisdiction of Indian courts. For example, in 1878, Judge Parker decided a case involving the theft of a horse committed by a non-Indian within Cherokee territory. Parker held in *Ex Parte Kenyon*[18] that the tribal court did not hold jurisdiction over the non-Indian defendant. "Focusing both on the unrelated sale of the horse in Kansas and on the defendant's race, Parker said: 'If there was any crime committed, at any time, it was committed not only beyond the place over which the Indian court had jurisdiction, but at the time it was committed by one over whose person such court did not have jurisdiction, because to give this court jurisdiction of the person of an offender, such offender must be an Indian, and the one against whom the offense is committed must also be an Indian.' ''[19]

There were some efforts promoting Indian self-government that were partially successful. In 1878, a bill to establish an Indian police force was introduced to Congress. This measure provided for the organization on reservations of police forces of trustworthy Indians, under the supervision of Indian agents. The program was greatly under-funded, but it succeeded because it met the needs of the Indian society.[20] Many other tribes already had similar police forces for the administration of law and order.

Another example of effective Indian self-government occurred on the Yakima Reservation. Here, the reservation was divided into five judicial districts by the Indian agent there. From these districts, elections were held for judges among tribal members. The agent found that, after a few years of experience, these Indian judges could try cases successfully. Some other attempts, however, to expand the powers of local Indian courts failed. "In 1878 the Society of Friends unsuccessfully presented Congress with a bill to establish a judicial system affecting all Indians except the Five Civilized Tribes. The Quaker proposal would have given jurisdiction over all criminal and civil cases arising on the reservation to courts on the reservation, presided over by the local federal Indian agent.[21] Further, the defendant would have a right to trial by a jury composed partly of Indians."[22]

The conflict over the extent of Indian court jurisdiction reached the Supreme Court in 1883. When Spotted Tail, a famous Sioux Indian, was killed by Crow Dog, equally famous, the matter was settled according to the Sioux code of justice. However, the whites were not satisfied with that Indian justice, and Crow Dog was prosecuted and convicted of murder in the United States Territorial Court for Dakota. This decision was appealed to the Supreme Court. The Supreme Court held in

Ex Parte Crow Dog[23] that the murder of one Indian by another Indian on the reservation was outside the criminal jurisdiction of a federal court. "The Supreme Court relied principally on the cultural differences between Indian and white society. After noting that action of the territorial court was unprecedented and legally insupportable, the court concluded: Indians are members of a community separated by race, tradition, instincts of a free though savage life, from the authority and power which seeks to impose upon them the restraints of an external and unknown code, and to subject them to the responsibilities of civil conduct, according to rules and penalties of which they could have no previous warning; which judges them by a standard made by others and not for them, which takes no account of the conditions which should exempt them from its exactions, and makes no allowance for their inability to understand it. . ."[24] In the *Ex Parte Crow Dog* case, it was another decision that supported Indian sovereignty.

Congress was quick to react after the *Ex Parte Crow Dog* decision.[25] After they overruled the Supreme Court, Congress further infringed upon tribal court jurisdictions by passing a series of statutes. Federal courts generally upheld such legislation, while at the same time upholding the sovereignty of the Indian nations in other cases. Indians themselves drew further away from federal policies as more measures designed to civilize the Indians were passed without consulting those people who were affected by them.

Congress responded to the public pressure following *Crow Dog* by passing the Act of March 3, 1885,[26] which made seven major crimes by Indians on a reservation, including the murder of one Indian by another, subject to federal jurisdiction. In this act, the federal courts were given jurisdiction over cases that had been earlier declared by the Supreme Court to be within the exclusive jurisdiction of the Indian courts. The Major Crimes Act placed the following seven crimes under federal jurisdiction: manslaughter, murder, rape, arson, burglary, assault with intent to kill, and larceny.

"Congress, under the Major Crimes Act sceme, preserves the idea that the tribe is the proper authority to regulate conduct [by defining crimes and then trying offenders] where fairly minor matters are involved. The tribal council and the tribal courts are almost reduced to municipal authority over petty offenses. The exercise of tribal sovereignty may take place without discomfort. The risk of defining and enforcing major crimes is too great to leave to chance enactment."[27]

The constitutionalists of the Major Crimes Act were challenged in *United States* v. *Kagama.*[28] "In *Kagama,* the Supreme Court held that the law was constitutional and made some revealing remarks which demonstrated both the frontier prejudices of that era and the patronizing attitude of the white man's government toward the Indians: 'Because of the local ill feeling, the people of the States where the Indians are found are often their deadliest enemies. From their very weakness and helpfulness, so largely due to the course of dealing of the federal government with them, and the treaties in which it has been promised, there arises the duty of protection, and with it the power. This has always been recognized by the Executive and by Congress, and by this court, whenever the question has arisen.' "[29]

The court, in noting that state jurisdiction had been excluded with regard to Indian inhabitants, went on to say: "The power of the General Government over these remnants of a race once powerful, now weak and diminishing in numbers, is necessary to their protection, as well as to the safety of those among whom they dwell. It must exist in that government because it has never existed anywhere else, because the theatre of its exercise is within the geographical limits of the United States, because it has never been denied, and because it alone can enforce its laws on all the tribes."[30] This is the basis of "plenary power"[31] which gives the United States jurisdiction over any territory within the United States that is not within the limits of a state, and over any offense committed within this territory whether by a white man or an Indian.

The Major Crimes Act, though representing Indian sovereignty to a degree, also represented a significant step toward assimilation of the Indian society. "*United States* v. *Whaley*[32] illustrated the change in the jurisdictional scheme brought about by the Major Crimes Act. The Indian defendants in *Whaley* were charged with the killing of Juan Baptiste, also an

Indian, on the Tule River Indian Reservation. The deceased was an Indian doctor, who, in the course of his treatment of tribal members, had been so unsuccessful as to induce the belief on the part of the tribe that he had been systematically poisoning his patients. Finally, one Indian, Hunter Jim, a favorite with the tribe, became seriously ill under the doctor's treatment. The members of the tribe held a council and informed the doctor that if Hunter Jim died, the doctor would also die. Jim did die, and a council was held and the four defendants were appointed to carry out the council's resolution. The next morning the doctor was shot. If this homocide had been committed prior to the passage of the Major Crimes Act, the federal court would have lacked jurisdiction. The tribal council, since it directed the acts of the defendants, would have granted an acquittal."[33] The Major Crimes Act was the first time that federal policy imposed American values on solely Indian matters on Indian land. The Act did not take into consideration the differences in the American and Indian systems of justice. American standards were implemented through the federal courts since the federal government restricted states from exerting their authority over crimes in Indian country.[34]

Conclusion

This chapter has examined the Constitution, the legislation of Congress, Indian sovereignty, and the problem of Indian jurisdiction with a focus on the legal status of Indian tribes in the United States. Andrew Jackson, in his State of the Union Address, outlined a plan to move the Indians westward to continue American expansion. This move was meant also to allow Indians to live peacefully and maintain their customs without outside influences or pressures. Jackson's plan was approved by Congress in the Indian Removal Act of 1830. This presented problems as the Indians resisted and led to much bloodshed on both sides.

At about the same time, the Indians were trying to maintain their sovereignty due, in part, to past treaties they had made with the United States. This led to two important cases,

Cherokee Nation v. *Georgia* and *Cherokee Nation* v. *Worcester,* which upheld Indian sovereignty. This was eventually overturned by Congress, who further limited tribal jurisdiction over their own matters when the Major Crimes Act of 1885 was passed. This put seven major crimes committed in Indian land under federal jurisdiction. This was challenged, unsuccessfully, in the case of *United States* v. *Kagama* in 1885. (Chapter 6 will focus on and examine the allocation of criminal jurisdiction in Indian country between the federal, state, and tribal governments.)

Criminal jurisdictional allocation in Indian country was actually formalized in the 1800s. Before that time, Indians had their own criminal codes and states often took jurisdiction over a crime if the crime was committed within its boundaries. However, there were certainly no clear cut approaches to jurisdiction.

The problems of the early 1800s, relating to sovereignty and legal rights of the Indians (i.e., *Worcester* v. *Georgia*), brought about a greater awareness of Indian problems associated with self-government and law and order. Though in the 1870s the Indian Affairs Commission recognized the strength of Indian codes of behavior, they did not appear strong enough to prevent problems related to criminal conduct on Indian land, including that of non-Indians. Therefore, solutions were sought from white society. In the court case, *Ex Parte Kenyon* in 1878, it was ruled that Indian courts did not have the authority to try non-Indians.

Self-government by Indian courts fell through also because the U.S. Government decided over which offenses Indian jurisdiction was allowed. This causes a loss of confidence in Indian government by the Indians and non-Indians and also meant that the Indian nation was not really self-governed. In the case *Ex Parte Crow Dog* in 1883, the Supreme Court ruled that the federal government did not have jurisdiction over one Indian murdering another Indian on Indian land. However, Congress quickly overruled them.

The jurisdiction of Indian courts was steadily eroding at this time. Further infringements of their authority came with the Major Crimes Act of 1885. This gave the federal courts jurisdiction over all major crimes committed on Indian land. This act is actually what set the tempo for the current division of criminal jurisdiction between the federal, state, and tribal governments. State jurisdiction and tribal jurisdiction were determined by federal authority and the powers of commerce. Public Law 280 of 1953, was the principal bill that actually shifted the federal government's power to some of the states. The Indian Reorganization Act of 1934 was the basis for the tribal government's power today.

Footnotes

Chapter 5

1. Meyer, William. *Native Americans: The New Indian Resistance,* Internaitonal Publishers, New York, 1971, p. 21.

2. Shaw, Ronald E. Andrew Jackson, "First Annual Message, December 8, 1829," *Oceana Publications,* Inc., New York, 1969, p. 26-28.

3. Act of May 28, 1830, Ch. 148, 4 Stat. 411.

4. Kickingbird, Kirk. "In Our Image. . . , After Our Likeness: The Drive For the Assimilation of Indian Court Systems," *American Criminal Law Review,* Vol. 13, No. 4 Sp. 76, p. 685.

5. *Ibid,* p. 687.

6. Meyer, p.22.

7. *Ibid,* p. 24.

8. Meyer, p. 24.

14. Kickingbird, p. 687.

15. Report of the Commissioner of Indian Affairs: Annual Report 1853, 249-250.

16. Hagan, W. Indian Police and Judges 11 (1966).

17. See Treaty with the Apache Tribe of July 1, 1852, Art. 8, 10 Stat. 979; Treaty with the Commanche, Kiowa, and Apache Tribes of July 27, 1853, Art. 3, 10 Stat. 1013 (1855).

20. Fritz, H. The Movement of Indian Assimilation, 20 (1963) at 140.

21. Id. at 216-217.

22. id.

26. Act of March 3, 1885, Ch. 341, Sec. 9, 23, Stat. 385, as amended, 18 U.S.C., Sec. 1153 (Supp. 1976).

27. Prince, Monroe E. *Law and the American Indian,* The Bobbs-Merrill Company, Inc., New York, 1973, p. 11.

29.   Kickingbird, p. 691.

30.   United States Department of the Interior, Federal Indian Law, United States Government Printing Office, Washington, 1958, p. 33.

31.   The plenary power over tribal relations and tribal property of the Indians has been often exercised by Congress. Sec. U.S. 218 (1897); and *Cherokee Nation* v. *Hitchcock,* 187 U.S. 294 (1902).

33.   *Immigration, Alienage and Nationality.* "Criminal Jurisdiction in Indian Country," University of California, Davis, Vol. 8, 1975, p. 443-444.

Cases

Chapter 5

9. 30 U.S. (5 Pet.) 1 (1831).
10. 30 U.S. (5 Pet.) (1831) at 17.
11. 31 U.S. (6 Pet.) 515 (1832).
12. Id. at 559.
13. Id. at 560–561.
14. Id. at 561.
18. 14 F. Cas. 353 (No. 7, 720) (C.C.W.D. Ark. 1878).
19. Id. at 355.
23. 109 U.S. 556 (1883).
24. Id. at 571.
25. 109 U.S. 556 (1883).
28. 118 U.S. 375 (1886).
29. Id. at 384.
30. 118. U.S. 375 (1886).
32. 37 F. 134 (C.C.S.J. Ca. 1888).
34. *Worcester* v. *Georgia*, 31 U.S. (6 Pet.) 515, 561 (1832).

Part II

Introduction

This book is an historical perspective of the criminal jurisdiction problems between the federal, state, and Indian courts concerning Indian land. Part I focused on the foundation of Indian-United States Government relations. This covered such important areas as the definition of an Indian, the Constitutional basis of U.S.-Indian relations, early Indian legislation, and problems with Indian sovereignty and assimilation. The first part of this research was important because it gives the reader a basic understanding of the foundation of U.S.-Indian relations. This foundation set the stage for the various legal transactions, and decisions made concerning Indians. Most of the major occurrences that have happened in the United States-United States Government-Indian relations have been illustrated by cases. Many of these cases were precedent-setting.

Part II will cover the criminal jurisdiction of Indian country and will focus on the federal, state, and tribal jurisdiction over crime and criminal conduct in Indian country. This section will also look at all the important court decisions and legislation that have had an effect on criminal jurisdiction of Indian country. Civil jurisdiction will also be briefly examined.

Chapter 6
Criminal Jurisdiction in Indian Country

The earlier chapters have studied how the jurisdictional arrangements between the federal, state, and tribal courts were set up. This was via legislation by Congress, the concept of United States sovereignty and its position as guardian over its ward (the Indians), the Constitutional power of commerce over Indians, aggressive westward expansion of the United States, United States recognition of partial Indian sovereignty, and Supreme Court decisions.

Historically, the U.S. Government has been interested not only in the expansion and control of its territory, but also in the protection of the Indian and his culture. This has been through assimilation of the Indians in part, and preservance of Indian sovereignty over their own affairs. With there being a thin line between assimilation and sovereignty, one area of major concern has been criminal jurisdiction in Indian country. It has been examined, in earlier chapters, how problems have arisen in trying to determine who has and should have criminal jurisdiction in Indian country. This is due to the concept of Indian sovereignty and long established criminal codes or rules of conduct in some tribes versus the U.S. position of jurisdiction over criminal conduct within its boundaries, yet outside of state boundaries, and the U.S. Government's position of guardian and protector over the Indians and Indian country. In the treaty years there were some statutes toward criminal jurisdictional allocation in Indian country; also there has been some earlier legislation by Congress with regard to criminal jurisdiction in Indian country.

Overall, the United States Government has controlled the jurisdictional allocation by Congress and Article I, Sec. 8, clause 3 of the Constitution and the commerce clause. The government's position has been to have jurisdiction over major criminal conduct in Indian country (the Major Crimes Act)[1] and allow Indian control over minor offenses. At the same time, the state has also wanted some jurisdiction over Indian affairs within its boundaries. This has been ruled against in some cases by the Supreme Court (*Worcester* v. *Georgia*).[2]

Despite the federal government's position toward jurisdiction in Indian country, there has been some problem and confusion with regard to the allocation of criminal jurisdiction in Indian country. This chapter will examine how criminal jurisdiction is determined and allocated in Indian country.

In determining who has criminal jurisdiction in Indian country, it is allocated to the federal government, the states, and to the Indian courts. This allocation is based on (1) the offense involved, (2) the races of the victim and the criminal offender, and (3) where the offense occurred. The question of who has Indian country jurisdiction between state and federal courts is rather simple—what would need to be determined is the offense involved. If it is a state offense, the state court has jurisdiction. If it is a federal offense, then jurisdiction belongs in the federal court. In these instances, it is irrelevant whether the offender is Indian or non-Indian. The real complication in jurisdictional issues occurs when tribal court jurisdiction of offenses on Indian reservations is considered.

Federal Jurisdiction

The federal government department that handles the affairs between the United States and the Indians is the Bureau of Indian Affairs (BIA). The BIA administers and coordinates the federal programs for the reservations and moved from the Department of War to the Department of the Interior in 1849.

All transactions between the United States wards, the Indian and non-Indians, are regulated through the Interior Department and the BIA. These include territorial disputes, land transactions, public health services, and schools.

A federal court has jurisdiction over all federal offenses. There are three exceptions to this. "The exceptions codified at 18 U.S.C. 1152,[3] provide that federal jurisdiction does not extend (1) to the offenses committed by one Indian against the person and property of another Indian, (2) to any Indian committing any offense in Indian country who has been punished under tribal law, and (3) to any case whereby stipulations of a treaty the exclusive jurisdiction over such offenses rests in the tribal court."[4] In connection with the exercise of federal criminal jurisdiction, Section 1152, of the Criminal Code, extends the general laws of the United States to Indian country, other than for those exceptions specified amongst the general laws in Section 1152 in the Assimilative Crime Statute.[5] In a recent Supreme Court decision, *William* v. *United States*,[6] the Assimilative Crime Statute has been held to be applicable to Indian country. "The effect of that statute is to incorporate the criminal laws of the several states into the laws of the United States so the violations will be prosecuted as federal offenses."[7] Despite these exceptions, 18 U.S.C. 1152, a separate statute, "the Major Crimes Act provides that a federal court has exclusive jurisdiction over thirteen named offenses even if the offenses are committed by an Indian in Indian country. These offenses are murder, manslaughter, rape, carnal knowledge as defined in the statute, assault with intent to rape, incest, assault resulting in serious bodily injury, arson, burglary, robbery, and larceny. An important exception to the Major Crimes Act is that a federal court does not have exclusive jurisdiction over the thirteen enumerated crimes if a state has validly assumed jurisdiction over crimes of an Indian reservation."[8]

"Federal courts, other than the Supreme Court, are courts of a limited jurisdiction.[9] Article III of the Constitution vests the judicial power of the United States 'in one Supreme Court, and in such inferior courts as the Congress may from time to time ordain and establish'. The lower federal courts constitute the 'inferior courts' thus authorized and they exercise only that criminal or civil jurisdiction which Congress has vested in them specifically by statutory law. Even that jurisdiction which has been vested in them can be withdrawn or limited at a later time by Congress."[10]

In its exercise of plenary power, Congress has largely excluded, until recent years, state jurisdiction. Because federal courts are of limited jurisdiction, in many instances a gap has appeared in jurisdiction.[11] This gap has been filled by tribal jurisdiction. This situation will prevail until other legislation is initiated by Congress which will place Indians in the same status as other United States citizens; that is, under the jurisdiction of the states in which they reside.[12]

"Juridictional problems may be statutorily adjusted, of course, by a state, and the United States where a state relinquishes jurisdiction over an Indian reservation within its borders, and the United States extends its jurisdiction generally to cover certain crimes within the limits of all Indian reservations, the intent of the state and the United States must be viewed in the light of the history, setting, and purpose of those jurisdictional acts."[13]

Congress gave its consent to all the states to assume criminal and civil jurisdiction over Indian country within their boundaries.[14] Jurisdiction was also granted to specific states, sometimes excluding certain Indian reservations.[15] This jurisdiction grant does not, however, give a state power to affect the federal trust status of personal property of Indians.[16]

"Since there is no federal common law of crimes, and because lower federal courts are courts of limited jurisdiction, a basis for the exercise of jurisdiction must be found in almost every instance in some applicable Federal Statute. Under certain circumstances, a de facto jurisdiction theretofore assumed and exercised by a state may be accorded great weight where Congress has not prescribed exclusive federal jurisdiction.[17] From the real standpoint of areas of application, the federal criminal statutes relating to Indian affairs generally are of two types: (a) those that apply regardless of the place of the offense,[18] and (b) offenses punishable by the United States only when committed within 'Indian country'.[19] Most of the federal statutes are of the latter type and are generally subject to further classification on the basis of subject matter or identity of person."[20]

State Jurisdiction

State jurisdiction over Indians and Indian country has been limited because of the Constitutional powers of the federal government. This can be seen in such cases as *Worcester* v. *Georgia*[21] and *United States* v. *Kagama.*[22]

When justice is effectively administered under state laws or by state law enforcement agencies, no Court of Indian Offenses will be established on an Indian reservation.[23] Jurisdictional conflicts may be statutorily adjusted, of course, by a state and federal government. "When a state relinquishes acquired jurisdiction on a reservation within that state, and the United States has, by law, extended its jurisdiction generally to certain crimes committed within the limits of 'any Indian reservation', the intent to assume jurisdiction must be viewed in the light of the history, setting and purpose of the general legislation."[24]

Federal statutes which grant or recognize state power over Indian affairs fall under two categories: (1) those that apply only to particular areas or tribes, and (2) those that apply throughout the United States. State laws and power have been extended by Congress to Indian reservations for probate matters involving allotments and laws enacted by Congress for covering health and educational conditions, and sanitation and quarantine regulations. A third area of state laws extended to Indian country is by the Assimilative Crime Act which makes a large number of offenses punishable in federal courts in accordance with state laws.[25]

State courts have criminal jurisdiction over all state offenses committed outside Indian land, regardless of the race of the offender. In addition, if the state has assumed jurisdiction pursuant to Public Law 280,[26] a state court has jurisdiction over all state offenses even if they are committed on Indian land. Public Law 280 was enacted by Congress in 1953. This was declared by the House Concurrent Resolution 108:

To be the policy of the federal government to, as rapidly as possible, make the Indians within the territorial limits of the United States subject to the same laws and entitled to the same privileges and responsibilities as are applicable to other citizens of the United States, to end their status as wards of the United States, and to grant them all the rights and prerogatives pertaining to American citizenship. The Act, as amended, gives Alaska, California, Minnesota (with one exception), Nebraska, Oregon (with one exception), and Wisconsin civil and criminal jurisdiction over Indian country. Section 7, of the Act, gives the concent of the federal government to any other state which would assume civil or criminal jurisdiction either by legislation or amendment of the state constitution, if required."[27]

Public Law 280 dealt with three groups of states in different ways, depending on the legal needs of the states. "Public Law 280 ceded criminal and civil jurisdiction directly to one group of states.[28] It empowered a second group of states to take jurisdiction over reservations by enactment of appropriate state legislation.[29] A third group of states could amend their state constitutions to assume such jurisdiction.[30] Despite its constitutionality,[31] Indian leaders severely criticized the Act for its destructive impact on tribal sovereignty.[32] Even in matters solely involving Indians within Indian territory, state law superseded the tribe's authority."[33]

Public Law 280 was vague, at best, and it was difficult to determine exactly what Congress meant by civil and criminal jurisdiction. It was assumed that the termination of federal jurisdiction now meant that the states held complete jurisdiction over Indians in Indian country. States under Section 7 of the Act, given the power to assume jurisdiction, felt that too many problems previously handled by the federal government would be transferred to the state. Therefore, many states refused to assume jurisdiction without adequate federal assistance to finance new and necessary programs, and also the requirement of tribal consent to state jurisdiction. As a result of pressure from tribes and Indian organizations, Public Law 280 was amended in the 1968 Civil Rights Act to add a tribal consent requirement to any new assumption or extension of state jurisdiction over Indians or Indian tribes. This Act also authorized states to be able to retrocede jurisdiction to the federal government, but only at the government's option. (Public Law 280 is one of the most severe pieces of federal government legislation in terms of impeding on tribal sovereignty.)

Much litigation has arisen from state attempts to extend jurisdiction over Indian country since Public Law 280 was enacted. Some of the general challenges regarding Public Law 280 include the fact that Public Law 280 has been challenged as unconstitutional on due process and equal protection grounds, because it does not apply uniformity to all Indians in the United States, and because it classifies persons on a tribal basis. Public Law 280 has also been challenged as an unconstitutional delegation of federal power to the states. However, these and other challenges have repeatedly been rejected by both federal and state courts. As far as the effect of Public Law 280 on tribal jurisdiction, it is a basic tenant of Indian law that Indian tribes maintain their internal sovereignty and jurisdiction except as it is expressly overridden by Congress.

Tribal Jurisdiction

A tribal court has jurisdiction over all of the offenses committed on the reservation which violate tribal law.[34] "Tribes may set up tribal courts according to their own practices and customs unless the federal government has withdrawn such authority from the tribes.[35] Most tribal codes limit jurisdiction to cases involving Indian offenders. If the state in which the reservation is located has assumed jurisdiction, the tribal court may have concurrent jurisdiction to the extent that tribal as well as state law has been violated."[36]

The current form of tribal government stems from the 1934 Indian Reorganization Act.[37] Even though this Act was not the first major piece of Indian legislation to emerge from the New Deal,[38] it has the most significant impact on tribal authority and self-government. Drafted by Felix S. Cohen, a Department of the Interior employee, who went on to publish the book *Federal Indian Law,* the act was permissive in nature, and could be rejected by any tribe.[39] The major features of the Act were, "the termination of allotment,[40] and the provision of federal legislative authority for tribal self-government.[41] Trusts created under the General Allotment Act were extended indefinitely,[42] all unallotted lands were restored to tribal ownership,[43] and the Secretary of the Interior was authorized to acquire land for tribes[44] and create new reservations.[45] The goal of the Act was to allow tribes to elect existance as separate people as an alternative to the mandatory assimilation of the General Allotment Act. The Act permitted those tribes who elected existence to adopt a constitution and bylaws for their self-government,[46] with certain enumerated powers in addition to any which might have existed under prior law."[47] These powers included negotiation with the federal, state, and local governments, employments of legal counsel, and the prevention of the sale or lease of tribal lands, or other tribal assets, without tribal consent. More important than just the end of allotment was the Act's provisions for tribal self-government. However, with this clearly being a legislative grant of power, it really gave Indians only limited powers of sovereignty subject to that legislation.

With regard to the Indian Reorganization Act, the tribal courts actually only have jurisdiction over those offenses which could be characterized as misdemeanors under state or federal law. The Indian Civil Rights Act of 1968,[48] puts a limit on the punishment which a tribal court may impose to a maximum imprisonment of six months or a fine of $500, or both.

Tribal court authority has been continually challenged in court. Federal courts, in some cases, have attempted to protect Indian sovereignty, only to be overruled by Congress. "In *Iron Crow* v. *Oglaula Tribe,*[49] the authority of tribal courts to impose criminal convictions for offenses against the tribal code was challenged on the grounds that there was no Constitutional or statutory authority for the jurisdiction of the Indian courts. The Eighth Circuit upheld the tribal court judgement, noting that the Constitution clearly recognizes the sovereignty of the Indian nations. Furthermore, the court said, 'sovereignty is absolute excepting only as to such rights as are taken away by the paramount government, the United States.'[50] The court went on to conclude that Congress had demonstrated a clear intention not to take away the jurisdictional rights challenged."[51]

The Tenth Circuit Court, in *Native American Church* v. *Navajo Tribal Council*,[52] upheld the force of Indian substantive laws. The court found that the First Amendment, the right to freedom of religion, applied only to the federal government and the states only by the Fourteenth Amendment and did not apply to Indian tribes. This was eventually overturned by Congress when it passed the 1968 Indian Civil Rights Act, of which Title I placed restraints on the tribal courts and governments by applying some of the language of the Bill of Rights to Indian tribes, including the due process and equal protection clauses.

The Supreme Court has found that tribal courts do not have authority over non-Indians. This was exemplified in *Oliphant* v. *Suguamish* Tribe[53] where the court held that tribal courts have no inherent authority to try and punish non-Indians.

In examining the tribal codes of law and order, it is not possible to mention them in the same respect as the United States Constitution or criminal codes, because there are many tribes and each one has its own regulations and customs. Many of them still have their own criminal codes for serious crimes such as murder, even though they are no longer applicable.[54] Basically, the only law and order codes that are applicable in tribal courts are those for misdemeanor violatins; this is in addition to the codes of civil conduct in which the tribal courts do assume jurisdiction.

An example of a tribal code would be that of the Navajo Tribe. In all civil cases, the Court of the Navajo Tribe follows any United States laws that are applicable. Matters that are not covered by traditional codes or United States laws are decided by the Court of the Navajo Tribe according to the laws of the state in which they occur. "(1) The Navajo Tribal Code, designated Volumes I and II, is at the present time, the only law that is and will be followed by the Courts of the Navajo Tribe in all cases litigated falling within their jurisdiction. (2) Though the Courts of the Navajo Tribe were granted specific authority by

Resolution C-09-58 to adopt rules, pleading, practice, or procedures by the Navajo courts that add to, that differ from, or that are in conflict with the Navajo Tribal Code. The Code is still the Supreme Law of Navajoland."[55]

This is an example of a tribel code that though an official code, is in reality a code of conduct under United States law. This is exemplified by using United States laws that are applicable here in civil tribal court cases. The tribal court has been more and more limited in actual authority to impose jurisdiction on any conduct within reservation boundaries. Even such things as civil matters and minor crimes are under tribal authority only because the United States chooses for it to be that way.

Conclusion

This chapter has examined the allocation of criminal jurisdiction in Indian country between the federal, state, and Indian courts. While the federal government was found to have limited power, they still appear to dictate the jurisdictional allocation here strictly by the Constitutional powers granted them. The Major Crimes Act gives the federal government jurisdiction over all major crimes committed on Indian land; the states have jurisdiction over state offenses. Public Law 280 gave specified states complete jurisdiction over Indian country within their territory and also gave other states the option of doing the same. Indian court jurisdiction is sometimes concurrent with state jurisdiction. In most cases, however, their jurisdiction has been limited to minor offenses.

Chapter 7 will outline the actual allocation of criminal jurisdiction of Indian country between the federal, state, and Indian courts.

Footnotes
Chapter 6

1. Act of March 3, 1885, Ch. 341, Sec. 9, 23, Stat. 385, as amended 18 U.S.C., Sec. 1153 (Supp. 1976).
3. 18 U.S.C., Sec. 1152 (1970).
4. Immigration, Alienage and Nationality. "Criminal Jurisdiction in Indian Country," University of California, *Davis Law Review,* Vol. 8, 1975, p. 436.
5. 18 U.S.C., 13.
7. Cohen, Felix. *Federal Indian Law,* p. 308.
8. *Criminal Jurisdiction in Indian Country,* p. 436, 18 U.S.C., 1153, 1970.
9. Harris, *The Judicial Power of the United States* (1940), p. 1.
10. Fourteenth Amendment, Federal Indian Law, United States Department of Interior, United States Government Printing Office, Washington: 1958, p. 307.
12. Fourteenth Amendment.
13. *Federal Indian Law,* p. 306.
14. See Section 7 of the Act of August 15, 1953, 57 Stat. 588, 28 U.S.C. 1360.
15. U.S.C. 1360, 54 Stat. 249, 18 U.S.C. 1162.
16. Op. Sol. M. 36362, August 13, 1954.
18. Ex., 18 U.S. 1158 and 1163.
19. Ex., 18 U.S.C. 1151, 1152, and 1153.
20. *Federal Indian Law,* p. 311.
23 25 C.F.R., 161.1 (c).
24. *Federal Indian Law,* p. 502.
26. 18 U.S.C., Sec. 1162 (1970); 28 U.S.C., Sec. 1360 (1970).

27. State Government, "The States and Indian Jurisdiction," by Leo Houston. Published by the Council of State Governments, Winter, 1977, p. 20.

28. U.S.C., Sec. 1360 (1970).

29. Act of August 15, 1953, Ch. 505, Sec. 6, 67 Stat. 589.

30. Act of August 15, 1953, Ch. 505, Sec. 7, 67 Stat. 389.

31. Public Law 280, 18 U.S.C., Sec. 1162 (1970); 28 U.S.C., Sec. 1360 (1970).

32. Wendell Chino; President of the National Congress of American Indians, "President Johnson Presents Message to Congress," Indian Records 28 (March 1968).

33. *Criminal Jurisdiction in Indian Country*, p. 437.

34. *Federal Indian Law*, 1 at 46.

35. Dowling, Criminal Jurisdiction Over Indians and Post-Conviction Remedies, 22 *Mont. L. Review*, 165, 171 (1961).

36. *Justice and the American Indian*, "Examination of the Basis of Tribal Law and Order Authority," Vol. IV, 9 (1974).

37. Act of June 18, 1934, Ch. 576, 48 Stat. 984.

38. The Indian Reorganization Act was preceded by the Johnson-O'Malley Act, 25 U.S.C., Sec. 452-54 (1970).

39. Act of June 18, 1934, Ch. 576, Sec. 18, 48 Stat. 984.

40. Id., Section 1.

41. Id., Section 16, Section 12.

42. Id., Section 2.

43. Id., Section 3.

44. Id., Section 5.

45. Id., Section 7.

46. Id., Section 16, Section 17.

47. Federick J. Martone. "American Indian Tribal Self-Government in the Federal System: Inherent Right or Congressional License?" *Notre Dame Lawyer*, April 1976, Vol. 51, No. 4, p. 613.

51. Kirk Kickingbird, "In Our Image. . . , After Our Likeness: The Drive For the Assimilation of Indian Court Systems," *American Criminal Law Review*, Sp. 76, Vol. 13, No. 4, p. 695.

55. Monroe E. Price, *Law and the American Indian*, Bobbs-Merrill Company, Incorporated, New York, 1973, p. 134.

Cases

Chapter 6

2. 31 U.S. (6 Pet.) 515 (1832).
6. 327 U.S. 711 (1946).
7. *U.S.* v. *Sosseur,* 181 F.2d 873, 874-875 (1950).
11. *Phillips* v. *Payne,* 92 U.S. 130; and *Ex Parte Ray,* 54, F. Supp. 218 (1943).
17. *Ex Parte Ray,* 54 F. Supp. 218 (1943).
21. 6 Pet. 515 (1832).
22. 118 U.S. 375 (1886).
25. *Williams* v. *United States,* 711 (1946).
47. 25 C.F.R., Section 11.2CA-11.21 (1974).
48. 25 U.S.C., Section 1302 (7) (1970).
49. 231 F.2d 89 (8th Cir. 1956).
50. Id. at 94.
51. Id. at 96.
52. 272 F.2d 131 (10th Cir. 1959).
53. 535 U.S. 191 (1978).
54. Major Crimes Act, 1885, Ch. 341, Sec. 9, 23, Stat. 385, at amended 18 U.S.C., Section 1153 (Supp. 1976).

Chapter 7
Government Establishment of Criminal Jurisdiction
in Indian Country

This chapter will focus on the specific criminal conduct in Indian country and who has jurisdiction.

Crimes In Indian Country

"As previously indicated, Congress defined 'Indian country' in 1948.[1] Before then, since the great bulk of the legislation penalized various acts committed on Indian reservations or within the Indian country, a question might arise in any given case whether an offense charged was in fact within the scope of the applicable legislation. The following general conclusions serve as guidelines to the historical development of the definition of 'Indian country': (1) Tribal land is considered 'Indian country' for purposes of Federal criminal jurisdiction.[2] (2) An allotment held under patent in fees and subject to restraint against alienation is likewise considered 'Indian country' for purposes of Federal criminal jurisdiction.[3] (3) An allotment held under trust patent, with title in the government, is likewise considered 'Indian country' during the trust period.[4] (4) Rights-of-way across the Indian reservation are considered 'Indian country' for some purposes of Federal criminal jurisdiction.[5] (5) It is questionable whether land held by an Indian under a fee patent without restriction is 'Indian country' for purposes of Federal criminal jurisdiction; the weight of authority is that the land is not 'Indian country' within the meaning of Federal penal statutes,[6] unless it is within the exterior boundaries of a reservation."[7]

There was a problem in determining jurisdiction, whether state or federal. Indians who were allotted were supposed to be under state jurisdiction since allotment terminated the tribal status and, therefore, federal jurisdiction. However, state law enforcement officers had trouble distinguishing patent in fee Indians from ward Indians. "In *Williams* v. *United States,*[8] it was held that the issuance by the United States of a fee simple patent to land or which an unemancipated Indian ward murdered another such Indian, did not remove that land from the reservation on the jurisdiction of the federal government. However, Circuit Judge Healy noted that, 'so far as presently concerns the Klamath and certain other reservations, it appears that Congress has since conferred upon state courts jurisdiction over crimes committed thereone.' "[9] In certain offenses, the nature of the offense along with the character of *locus in quo* determine federal jurisdiction without regard to the question of whether the offender or the victim is an Indian.[10] In other offenses, among other things, jurisdiction depends upon the persons involved.

Crimes in Indian Country by Indians Against Indians

Those offenses committed by an Indian against another Indian in Indian country are normally within tribal court jurisdiction.[11] "In determining whether an offense by an Indian against an Indian falls within the jurisdiction of tribal courts, we look to federal laws and treaties largely for the limitations on tribal authority. The importance of such limitations stems from the Act of March 3, 1885.[12] This Act brought under federal jurisdiction certain offenses committed by Indians against Indians, notably murder, manslaughter, rape, assault with intent to kill, arson, burglary, and larceny. In later years robbery, incest, and assault with a dangerous weapon were added to this list."[13] Some other federal statutes relating to non-Indian or

Indians are applicable to offenses by Indians committed on an Indian reservation.

The federal courts have exclusive jurisdiction over murder or manslaughter on Indian reservations and the tribal courts may not act to punish a member of the tribe who has killed another member.[14] The policy of the federal government with regard to tribal jurisdiction over offenses between Indians is embodied in a series of statutes starting with the Act of March 3, 1817.[15]

Crimes in Indian Country by Non-Indians Against Indians

In general, offenses committed by non-Indians against Indians are punishable in federal courts where the offense is specified in the federal code of territorial offenses. Federal jurisdiction over non-Indian offenders against Indians was initially put on a statutory basis by the first Trade and Intercourse Act, the Act of July 22, 1790[16] (Chapter 3). Subsequent statutes reenacted this provision with the general rule of the Act being confirmed by the Act of March 3, 1817.[17] "The Trade and Intercourse Act of June 30, 1834,[18] reenacted the rule developed in the earlier statutes. This rule was subsequently incorporated in the revised statutes as Section 2145, now 18 U.S.C. 1152 and 1153. The exceptions contained in Section 1152 relating to offenses by Indians against Indians and to offenders punished by tribal law have no application to offenses committed by non-Indians against Indians. The third exception in Section 1152, dealing with the case of a treaty where the exclusive jurisdiction over such offenses is secured to the Indian tribes might have current application, but no such treaty provisions appear to be now in force."[19] Except for the general statutes, Congress every now and then has enacted various laws to punish particular offenses committed by non-Indians against Indians within Indian country.[20]

Crimes in Indian Country by Indians Against Non-Indians

"An Indian committing offenses in the Indian country against non-Indian is subject to the Act of March 3, 1885,

Section 9,[21] which with an amendment, became Section 328 of the United States Criminal Code of 1910 and now is Section 1153 of Title 18 of the United States Code,[22] providing for the prosecution in the federal courts of Indians committing within Indian reservations any of ten specifically mentioned offenses whether against Indians or against non-Indians."[23] Apart from those ten crimes, an Indian committing offenses in Indian country against a non-Indian is subject to the Federal Code of Territorial Offenses.[24] There are two exceptions to this: "(a) Where he 'has been punished by the local law of the tribe' and (b) 'whereby treaty stipulations, the exclusive jurisdiction over such offenses is or may be secured to the Indian tribes respectively.' "[25] The Act of March 3, 1817,[26] was the first federal enactment dealing generally with crimes by Indians against non-Indians in Indian country. "This provision was subsequently incorporated in Section 25 of the Trade and Intercourse Act of 1834,[27] and became part of Section 3 of the Act of March 27, 1854,[28] from which Section 2145 of the Revised Statutes and 18 U.S.C. 1152 and 1153 were derived."[29]

Crimes in Areas within Exclusive Federal Jurisdiction

"Section 1152, Title 18,[30] extends to Indian reservations, with exceptions already noted, the general laws of the United States as to the punishment of crimes committed in any place within the sole and exclusive jurisdiction of the United States, except the District of Columbia. While the federal criminal law may seem meager and inadequate when compared to some state codes, it is supplemental by the Assimilative Crimes Statute,[31] which makes acts, not made penal by any other laws of Congress, committed upon land within the exclusive jurisdiction of the United States subject to federal prosecution wherever made criminal by state law. Thus, state criminal provisions can be enforced in the absence of applicable federal law. If the act committed on an Indian reservation is a crime under federal law, it must be prosecuted, of course, under that law—not under state law."[32]

Crimes in Which Locus is Irrelevant

There are certain federal offenses with regard to Indian affairs, such as making prohibited contracts with Indian tribes,[33] purchasing I.D. cattle without permission,[34] and stealing or embezzling from Indian tribal organizations,[35] that are under federal jurisdiction regardless of the place of the offense.

Crimes in Indian Country by Non-Indians Against Non-Indians

In general, offenses committed by a non-Indian against a non-Indian in Indian country are punishable by the state[36] for criminal jurisdiction, in situations where Indians are not involved, an Indian reservation is normally considered to be a part of the state within which it is located.[37]

Conclusion

This chapter has examined the actual jurisdiction allocation of the federal, state, and tribal courts concerning Indian land. The result is that it is a complex and inconsistent set-up with regard to jurisdiction of Indian country. This jurisdiction is divided amongst the federal, state, and tribal courts on the basis of three variables: races of the offender and victim, the nature of the offense, and the title or status of the land in which the offense occurred.

Chapter 8 will examine, in brief, the allocation of civil jurisdiction and some of the related factors connected with it. As a general practice, the United States Government does not concern itself with civil disputes concerning Indians against Indians within Indian territory. However, there is a civil jurisdiction allocation that contains two suites against or by the Government concerning Indians. In terms of time, the civil jurisdiction allocation began in the early 1800s and is concurrent with criminal jurisdictional allocation.

Footnotes

Chapter 7

1.   18 U.S.C. 1151.

5   18 U.S.C. 1151 et Seq.

7.   *Federal Indian Law.* United Stated Department of Interior, United States Government Printing Office, Washington: 1958, p. 310.

9.   215 F 2d. 1, p. 3, citing 67, Stat. 588 (1954), *Federal Indian Law,* p. 318.

11.   18 U.S.C. 1152.

12.   23 Stat. 362, 385, now 18 U.S.C. 1151 and 1153.

13.   Act of March 4, 1909, Sec. 328, 35 Stat. 1088, 1151; Act of June 28, 1932, 47 Stat. 336, 337, *Federal Indian Law,* p. 320.

15.   3 Stat. 383, now covered by 18 U.S.C. 1152.

16.   Secs. 5 and 6, 1 Stat. 137, 138.

17.   Stat. 383.

19.   *Federal Indian Law,* p. 324.

20.   See 18 U.S.C. Ch. 53, Secs. 437–439.

21.   23 Stat. 362, 385, 18 U.S.C. 1153.

23.   *Federal Indian Law,* p. 321.

24.   18 U.S.C, 1151, 1152.

25.   *Federal Indian Law,* p. 322.

26.   3 Stat. 383.

27.   Act of June 30, 1834, 4 Stat. 729, 733.

28.   10 Stat. 269, 270.

29.   *Federal Indian Law,* p. 324.

30.   June 30, 1834, Sec. 25, 4 Stat. 733, as amended by the Act of March 27, 1854, Sec. 3, 10, Stat. 269, 270, R.S. Sec. 2145.

31. R.S. Sec. 5391; act of July 7, 1898, Sec. 2, 30 Stat. 717, Act of March 4, 1909, Sec. 289, 35 Stat. 1089, 1145, now 18 U.S.C. 13.

32. *Federal Indian Law,* p. 325.

33. Act of March 3, 1871, Sec. 3, 16, Stat. 544, 570; R.S. Sec. 2105, 18 U.S.C. 438.

34. Act of March 3, 1865, Sec. 8, 13, Stat. 541, 563.

35. Act of August 1, 1956, 70 Stat. 792, 18 U.S.C. 1163.

Cases

Chapter 7

2. *Bates* v. *Clark*, 95 U.S. 204 (1877).

3. *United States* v. *Ramsey*, 271 U.S. 467 (1926); *Toosigah* v. *United States*, 137 F.2d, 713 (1943).

4. *United States* v. *Sutton*, 215 U.S. 291 (1909); *Hallowell* v. *United States*, 221 U.S. 317 (1911); *United States* v. *Pelican*, 232 U.S. 442 (1914); *Ex Parte Pero*, 99 F.2d 28 (1938); *Ex Parte Van Moore*, 221 Fed. 95A (1915); and *Toorsgah* v. *United States*, supra.

6. CF. *Eugene Sol Lovie* v. *United States*, 274 Fed. 47 (1921); 60 I.D. 368, 3369; *Williams* v. *United States*, 215 F.2d 1 (1954); *State* v. *Monroe* 556, 274 Pac. 840 (1929), U.S.C. 1151; *Irvine* v. *District Court*, 239 P. 2d, 272 (1951).

8. 215 F.2d 1 (1954).

10. *United States* v. *Sutton*, 215 U.S. 291, 295 (1909). Accod: *Perrin* v. *United States*, 232 U.S. 478 (1914).

14. *United States* v. *Whaley*, 37 Fed. 145 (1888).

22. Gon-Shay-Ee, Petitioner, 130 U.S. 343 (1889).

23. *Appapas* v. *United States*, 233 U.S. 587 (1914).

36. *United States* v. *McBratney*, 104 U.S. 621 (1881). New York ex ref. *Ray* v. *Martin*, 326 U.S. 496 (1946).

37. *Draper* v, *United States*, 164 U.S. 240 (1896).

Chapter 8
Civil Jurisdiction in Indian Country

Jurisdiction, as applied to the courts, is the power of a court to hear matters of a justifiable nature arising within the limits to which the judicial power of those courts extends.

Federal Courts

The judicial power of the United States is in the Supreme Court as well as lower courts. The power comes from the United States Constitution, Article I, Clause 8, Section 3. "In considering the jurisdiction of the federal courts, it may be observed that under the Constitution[1] and laws[2] of the United States the federal courts exercise jurisdiction in two different classes of cases—cases where the jurisdiction depends upon the character of the parties, and cases where the jurisdiction depends upon the subject matter of the suit."[3] Jurisdiction dependent upon the parties includes the United States as the plaintiff, the United States as the defendant, the United States as intervener; Indian tribe as party litigant, and the individual Indian as party litigant.

A. Jurisdiction Dependent on Parties

1. *The United States as plaintiff:* "It may be stated as a general proposition that under Section 1331 et. seq. of Title 28

of the United States Code, the District Courts of the United States have jurisdiction of all suits of a civil nature, at common law or in equity, in which the United States is the plaintiff."[4]

2. *The United States as defendant:* The general rule here is that the United States cannot be sued in any court, whether federal or state, without its consent.[5] This consent has been granted with regard to a tort claim which accrued on or after January 1, 1945.[6] This is also available to the individual Indian.[7]

3. *United States as intervener:* The question arises as to whether the United States can become a party to a pending suit by intervention in view of the established doctrine that the United States cannot be sued without its consent. "It appears that where an intervention places the government in the position of plaintiff, as in *New York* v. *New Jersey*,[8] and *Oklahoma* v. *Texas*,[9] the government may properly become an intervener. It is clear, however, that if by such intervention the government would become virtually a defendant in the suit, its appearance as an intervener would come in dire conflict with the ruling that the United States cannot be sued. The consent of the United States cannot be given by any officer of the United States unless authority to do so has been conferred upon by him by some act of Congress."[10]

4. *Indian tribe as party litigant:* Though the Indian tribes in the United States territory have some degree of sovereignty, they have been declared by the Supreme Court not to be states of the Union, or "foreign nations" within the meaning of Article III, Section 2, of the United States Constitution. This gives original jurisdiction to the Supreme Court in any controversy in which a state or one of its citizens is a party thereof, and a foreign state and its citizens thereof are parties.[11] As a result, an Indian tribe, as such, cannot be sued, or sue, or intervene in any case in which the original jurisdiction of the Supreme Court is invoked.[12]

5. *Individual Indian as party litigant:* "As a general rule, an Indian, irrespective of his citizenship or tribal relations, may sue in any state court of competent jurisdiction to redress any wrong committed against his person or property outside the limits of the reservation.[13] But the mere fact that the plaintiff

is an Indian does not vest jurisdiction in the federal courts.[14] This being true, the only grounds upon which a federal court could take jurisdiction of a suit by an Indian would be either because of diversity of citizenship between the plaintiff and defendant or because the cause of action arose under the Constitution, treaties, or laws of the United States."[15]

B. Jurisdiction Dependent upon Character of Subject Matter

"As to the character of the subject matter as an element of federal jurisdiction, it is to be observed that the cases are considerably in conflict in determining whether an action arises under the Constitution, treaties, or laws of the United States. It is quite clear, however, that the federal question must appear by specific allegations in the bill of complaint, and not from facts developed either in the answer or in the course of the trial.[16] A number of general statutes contain jurisdictional provisions conferring jurisdiction over defined subjects of Indian concern upon the Federal courts.[17] Other statutes contain provisions conferring jurisdiction over various matters upon territorial courts or courts of the United States in the territories."[18] In addition, there are several special statutes containing jurisdictional provisions relating to specific subjects.[19]

Other courts concerning Indian civil jurisdiction are the Court of Claims, the Indian Claims Commission, the Federal Administrative Tribunals, the State Courts, and the Tribal Courts.

Court of Claims

While the United States cannot be sued without its consent, it can be sued with its consent. This consent may be conditional: "Conditioned on the requirement that all sums expended gratuitously by the United States for the benefit of the tribe or band shall be offset against the amount found due.[20]

The burden is on the United States, however, to show that the expenditures were gratuities,[21] and on the court to specify which gratuities are offset against the judgment.[22] So far as the Court of Claims is concerned, its jurisdiction rests upon these general proportions, and therefore the extent of the jurisdiction is to be measured by the provisions of the jurisdictional act of Congress by which it is conferred in particular instances where such jurisdiction is invoked."[23] In other words, the Court of Claims does not have any general jurisdiciton over claims against the United States.[24]

Indian Claims Commission

"In creating a temporary three-member Indian Claims Commission, Congress provided in connection with Indian claims arising prior to August 13, 1946,[25] a forum for suits against the United States by any 'identifiable group'[26] of Indian claimants residing in the United States or Alaska covering (1) claims in law or equity,[27] (2) tort claims,[28] (3) claims based on the taking of land without payment of the agreed compensation.[29]"[30] The Indian Claims Commission was authorized to establish an investigation division. This division would search for all evidence affecting each claim.[31]

Federal Administrative Tribunals

The judicial power of the federal government is vested in the Supreme Court by the United States Constitution. Despite this fact, there are some matters which relate to the execution of Congressional powers by other provisions of the Constitution which are susceptible of judicial determination. For these types of matters, Congress may use its own options as to whether or not to bring the matters within the cognizance of Federal courts.[32] Congress may refer to these matters to special tribunals if it will be helpful or essential to execute powers delegated to it by the Constitution. When a matter is exclusively before a tribunal due to an act of Congress, the federal courts have no jurisdiction to reexamine it for errors.[33] The judgment of a special tribunal given the power to pass upon judicial questions cannot be attacked for mistake or fraud unless it is proved that it would prevent a full hearing.[34]

State Courts

"In matters not affecting either the federal government or the tribal relations, an Indian has the same status to sue and be sued in state courts as any citizen.[35] In matters affecting either the federal government or the tribal relations, Congress has the power, of course, to vest jurisdiction in state courts, if it so desires. Limited civil jurisdiction already has been granted to some states,[36] and section 7 of the Act of August 15, 1953,[37] constituted a standing offer of federal consent to states to assume jurisdiction."[38] The state courts have no jurisdiction in those civil matters affecting tribal relations or restricted property of the Indians unless provided otherwise by Congress, as long as the United States retains governmental control over them. Other areas in which the State could assume jurisdiction under certain conditions, such as federally approved, are questions of jurisdiction concerning determining heirs and partitions of allotted land controversies.

Tribal Courts

The Federal Constitution gave Congress the power to regulate commerce with Indian tribes.[39] This also served as recognition that sovereignty existed in the Indian tribes; since Congress has not withdrawn it, a quasi-sovereignty still remains in the tribal courts. The authority of those courts find their statutory support in Title 25, U.S. Code, Section 2, as well as other Congressional appropriations made for Indian courts.[40] An Indian tribe has the power to confer upon the jurisdiction of its own court for controversies involving Indians and decisions rendered by tribal courts in cases properly within their jurisdiction are recognized.[41]

There is always the question as to how far the power to confer upon tribal court jurisdiction has been exercised. This matter has been left primarily to the tribes themselves. "One of the few federal statutes which appears to recognize tribal jurisdiction over civil cases is Section 229 of Title 25 of the United States Code.[42] This statute provides that where injuries to property are committed by an Indian, application for redress shall be made by the appropriate federal authorities 'to the nation or tribe to which such Indian shall belong, for satisfaction'. It has been noted by the Solicitor for the Interior Department[43] that this provision assumes that the Indian tribe has the means of compelling return of stolen property or other forms of satisfaction where its members have violated the rights of non-Indians."[44]

Aside from this general status, there was a special provision made by federal law with respect to the tribal courts in the Indian Territory. "The jurisdiction of these courts, both in civil and in criminal matters, over Indians belonging to the same tribe, was specifically recognized by the Act of May 2, 1890,[45] which provided for a temporary government for the Territory of Oklahoma and enlarged the jurisdiction of the United States court in the Indian Territory. Under sections 30 and 31 of this Act, the exclusive jurisdiction preserved to the judicial tribunals of the Indian nations in all civil and criminal cases was limited to those cases in which 'members of said Nations' were the sole parties, which creates an ambiguity as to the meaning of the words 'only parties' or 'sole parties.' "[46]

Conclusion

This chapter examined the civil jurisdiction allocation of Indian country. For the federal courts, the jurisdiction is dependent upon the parties and upon the character of the subject matter. For federal jurisdiction, dependent upon parties, the jurisdiction depends upon the United States as plaintiff, defendant, intervener, and Indian tribes as party litigant, or an individual Indial as part litigant. Other areas of civil jurisdiction vary depending upon whether it is written the Court of Claims, the Indian Claims Commission, the Federal Administrative Tribunals, the State Courts, and the Tribal Courts. This chapter has examined the civil jurisdiction allocation of Indian country and the important cases on legislation that pertain to it.

Chapter 9 will focus on American Indian sovereignty in both the eyes of the Indians and the federal government. American Indian sovereignty, and the problems surrounding it, has existed since the English settlers first arrived on North American soil. Indian sovereignty claim is really the basis for the gap between Indians and the United States. By right, or perhaps because they were here first, Indians may have a claim to being sovereign. However, they are not recognized internationally as sovereign. When non-Indians took control of this territory, mostly through force, they actually became the sovereign of this land.

Indians have fought for their own sovereignty within the United States limits throughout American history. This effort has been met with continual resistance dating back to the treaty years of the 1700s and 1800s. The sovereignty of Indians as an independent unit has been partially recognized and at the same time denied through such measures as the Indian Removal Act of 1830 and the Indian Reorganization Act of 1934. Sovereignty has been fought for and tested in many court cases. The two most famous cases are *Worcester* v. *Georgia*, 1832, and *Cherokee Nation* v. *Georgia*, 1831. These cases affirmed the sovereignty of the Indian nations as a whole, but within the sovereign authority of the United States within this territory.

In retrospect, the United States is the actual sovereign within United States territory, because they accept their relationship to the Indians as that of a guardian to its ward. However, the Indians have some degree of sovereignty within their own culture and outside that of the United States culture. There will be a continual struggle and resistance by the Indians until they realize such rights as hunting and fishing, etc., uninterrupted.

Footnotes

Chapter 8

1. Art. III, Sec. 2, The Constitution of the Untied States.
2. 28 U.S.C.A. 1331 et. seq.
3. *Federal Indian Law.* United States Department of the Interior, United States Government Printing Office, Washington: 1958, p. 327.
4. *Ibid.,* p. 336.
6. 28 U.S.C. 1346 (b), 2401 (b) and 2671 et. seq.
10. *Federal Indian Law,* p. 340.
15. *Ibid.,* p. 343.
17. Act of June 30, 1834, 4 Stat. 729, 733, 734; Act of March 30, 1802, 2 Stat. 139, 145.
18. Idaho Territory: Act of July 3, 1882, Stat. 148; *Federal Indian Law,* p. 342.
19. Act of June 9, 1892, 27 Stat; 768.
20. Sec. 25 U.S.C. 475.
23. *Federal Indian Law,* p. 344.
30. *Ibid.,* p. 356.
31. 25 U.S.C. 70.
36. 28 U.S.C. 1360, 25 U.S.C. 233.
37. 67 Stat. 589, 28 U.S.C. 1360 note.
38. *Federal Indian Law,* p. 363.
39. Constitution, Art. I, Sec. 8, cl. 3.
42. R.S. Sec. 2156, derived from Act of June 30, 1834, Sec. 17, 4 Stat. 729, 731.
43. 55 I.D. 14, 63 (1934).
44. *Federal Indian Law,* p. 368.
45. 26 Stat. 81.
46. *Federal Indian Law,* p. 371.

Cases

Chapter 8

4.　*United States* v. *Board of County Commissioners of Grady County, Oklahoma*, 54 F.2d 593 (1931).

5.　*Kansas* v. *Colorado*, 206 U.S. 46, 82 (1907); *Kawanakoa* v. *Polybland, Trustee*, s.c. 205 U.S. 349.

7.　*Hatahley et al.* v. *United States*, 351 U.S. 173, 181 (1956).

8.　256 U.S. 296 (1921).

9.　258 U.S. 574 (1922).

10.　*Stanley* v. *Schualby*, 162 U.S. 255 (1896).

11.　*Cherokee Nation* v. *Georgia*, 5 Pet. 1 (1831).

12.　*Yankton Sioux Tribe* v. *United States*, 272 U.S. 351 (1926).

13.　*Wiley* v. *Keorkirk*, 6 Kan. 94, 110 (1870), *Brown* v. *Anderson*, 610 Okla. 136, 160 Pac. 724.

14.　*United States* v. *Seneca Nation of New York Indians*, 274 Feb. 946, 950 (1921).

15.　*Deere* v. *St. Lawrence River Power Company*, 32 F.2d 550 (1929).

16.　*Shulthis* v. *McDougel*, 225 U.S. 561 (1922).

21.　*Seminole Nation* v. *United States*, 102 Ct. Cl. 565 (1944).

22.　*Seminole Nation* v. *United States*, 316 U.S., 286, 308 (1942).

23.　*DeGroot* v. *United States*, 5 Wall. 419 (1866); *Ex Parte Russell*, 13 Wall. 664 (1871); *McElrath* v. *United States*, 102 U.S. 426 (1880).

24.　*Thruston* v. *United States*, 232 U.S. 469, 476 (1914); Citing *Johnson* v. *United States*, 160 U.S. 546, 549 (1896).

25.　*Choctaw Nation* v. *United States*, 118 F. Suppl. 365 (1954).

26.　*Thompson* v. *United States*, 122 Ct. Cl. 348 (1952); 60 I.D. 152.

27.　*Otoe and Missouri Tribe of Indians* v. *United States*, 131 F. Supp. 265 (1955).

28.　*Osage Nation* v. *United States*, 97 F. Supp. 381 (1951).

29.   25 U.S.C. 70a, 70b, *Otoe and Missouri Tribe of Indians* v. *United States,* op. cit. supra.

32.   *Murray's Lessee* v. *Hoboken Land and Improvement Company,* 18 How. 272 (1855).

33.   *Hallowell* v. *Commons,* 239 U.S. 506, 508 (1916).

34.   *United States* v. *Wunderlih et. al.,* 342 U.S. 98 (1951).

35.   *Felix* v. *Patrick,* 145 U.S. 317, 332 (1892).

40.   *Iron Crow et. al.* v. *Oglala Sioux Tribe of Pine Ridge Reservation,* 231 F.2d 89, 92 ff. (1956).

41.   *Standley* v. *Roberts,* 59 F. 836 (1894); *Raymend* v. *Raymond,* 83 F. 721 (1897).

46.   *Alberty* v. *United States,* 162 U.S. 466 (1896).

Part III

Introduction

Part II studied the allocation of criminal jurisdiction in Indian country. It examined the individual roles that the federal, state, and tribal courts played in criminal jurisdiction in Indian country. It also examined important legislation and cases that were instrumental in determining jurisdictional allocation. Civil jurisdiction was also looked at. This jurisdiction varies and is dependent upon the parties involved, the subject matter, and the court.

Part III will examine Indian sovereignty and various related areas such as civil rights, Indian resistance, self-determination, etc. Part II will also look at the problems in the jurisdictional set-up, what some of the criticisms of this set-up are, and what solutions can be afforded. A personal opinion of the entire subject matter will be the focus of the last Chapter in this section, as I will examine my view of the jurisdictional set-up and what I see as alternatives to the present system.

Chapter 9
The Scope of Indian Sonvereignty

American Indian sovereignty has been examined throughout the first eight chapters in terms of defining it, assessing it legitimately, viewing its relation to the United States and the United States government, viewing its recognition in terms of the United States Constitution, Supreme Court, and lower court cases.

This chapter will focus on actual American Indian sovereignty in terms of tribal self-government, rights, and United States recognition. First of all, the chapter will examine the concept of Indian sovereignty in terms of international law and recognition.

International Law

Initially, European citizens travelled to North America, discovered it, established settlements on it, made claims to it for their sovereign nations, and engaged in war with the native inhabitants. In 400 years, the conquest of North America was complete. Without a doubt, the American colonists represented the sovereignty of their mother country, Great Britain. Equally true is the fact that the various Indian tribes were sovereign states.[1] Certainly, before the Europeans arrived, the tribes exercised total self-government over the lands they occupied

93

without outside influence. What effect, in this case, did the European "discovery" and conquest have on the status of Indian tribes within the doctrine of international law?

"A state can acquire sovereignty over territory in various ways, two of which are conquest and cession.[2] A state acquires sovereignty over the territory of another state by conquest under two sets of circumstances: (a) where the territory annexed has been conquered or subjugated by annexing state, (b) where the territory annexed is in a position of virtual subordination to the annexing state at the time the latter's intention of annexatin is declared. . .Conquest of a territory as under (a) is not sufficient to constitute acquisition of title; there must be, in addition, a formally declared intention to annex.[3]

"On the other hand, a state acquires sovereignty over the territory of another state by cession, when the ceding state transfers its territory to the acquiring state: Cession rests on the principle that the right of transferring its territory is a fundamental attribute of the sovereignty of a state. The cession of a territory may be voluntary, or it may be made under compulsion as a result of a war conducted successfully by the state to which the territory is to be ceded. As a matter of fact, a cession of territory following defeat in war is more usual than annexation."[4]

When you apply these general international rules to the historical reality of Britain, and later American claims to the United States, it becomes clear that the effect of cession and conquest leaves the Indian tribes with no internationally recognizable claim to sovereignty over any part of the territory now a part of the United States. The truth is that the Indian tribes were conquered, subjugated, and more or less put into a position of virtual subordination. The United States has declared an intent to annex the lands it claimed; those lands not taken in combat were involuntarily or voluntarily ceded to the United States by treaty and agreement.

"At least one international tribunal is in accord. In the case of Cayuga Indian claims [*Great Britain* v. *United States*],[5] Great Britain attempted to sue the United States on behalf of the Cayuga Indian Nation. The tribunal held that the claim could not be maintained on behalf of the Cayuga Nation, but only 'on behalf of the Cayuga Indians in Canada', because the Cayuga Nation, 'an Indian tribe [many of whose members were in the state of New York, not in Canada]. . .is not a legal unit of international law.' "[6]

It has been determined that Indian tribes are not recognized as internationally as sovereign. We have also realized, through the earlier chapters, that the United States is actually the real sovereign power of this territory and only respects Indians sovereignty to a very small degree. Nonetheless, let us examine Indian sovereignty in the United States more closely.

Civil Rights

In terms of civil rights under tribal government, Indian tribes do have some degree of sovereignty. However, it is sovereignty that is given to them by the federal government.

Santa Clara Pueblo v. *Martinez,*[7] decided in 1978, was the first Supreme Court review of the Indian Civil Rights Act of 1968.[8] "The Indian Civil Rights Act reflected a majoritarian view[9] that all Indian tribal governments must be required to respect the rights and liberties of persons coming under their authority.[10] While Indian tribes are not bound by the United States Constitution,[11] they are bound by acts of Congress, which have been held to have plenary authority over them.[12] Consequently, the Indian Civil Rights Act, which makes the Constitutional guarantees of liberty and property binding on Indian tribes, has the effect of creating new rights against tribal governments. Strictly speaking, it is inaccurate to call them Constitutional rights, since they derive from statute. The statute repeats the language of the Constitution, however, and covers most of the rights and liberties found there,[13] with some notable exceptions. These exceptions were intended to avoid infringing upon the rights of tribes to preserve their identity and cultural autonomy."[14]

In viewing the tribal court system, sharp contrasts are apparent. The existence of most tribal courts comes from the tribe's legislative bodies.[15] Tribal constitutions generally assign the central role in tribal government to the tribal council rather than providing for co-equal branches. Tribal courts are, overall, the creation of ordinances enacted by the tribal council.[16] As a result, there exists a different relationship between the judiciary and legislature in Indian and American governments. The roles of tribal courts in tribal government have been, historically, fairly limited. In addition, not many of the tribal judges have had any formal training in law. This has a great impact on the respect of tribal members and other agencies of tribal government for the tribal courts.[17]

How can one better understand how the American systems and influence also impinge on Indian sovereignty? Though the Indian government and court system may not be on the same level as the United States system in terms of sophistication, and education, it is apparent that the Indians themselves feel the United States presence in determining their own acceptance of Indian government.

Bureau of Indian Affairs

In observing Indian resistance today, one area in which the Indians have had problems is with the Bureau of Indian Affairs. While their role, historically, is supposed to be one of protecting the Indians, it is actually the source of the greatest exploitation of the Indians. The Indians have little to say regarding their own services or property. All transactions between Indians and non-Indians are regulated through the Bureau of Indian Affairs. The problems of the Indians go on and on: Infant mortality is twice that of the rest of America; there is a 50% high school dropout rate, life expectancy on an Indian reservation is only 43 years. . . .These are hardly statistics with which one could be satified. Since the Bureau of Indian Affairs runs all of the Indian affairs, it seems apparent that something is wrong.

Land and Water Rights

In the original treaties with the various Indian nations, the United States Government guaranteed these nations the utilization and possession of both water and land. Under the terms of the treaties, the federal government was legally obligated to protect Indian possessions from violations by state and local authorities and private citizens. Nevertheless, the government has not provided this protection. Not only that, but the federal government itself has violated the treaty rights. Presently, there are many tribes waging legal battles for control over their rightful lands and waters. The following case is a sample of such a legal battle.

"The Seminole: in Florida, as in California, the United States Claims Commission has recognized Indian title to 80% of the state. The Seminole tribe, though it made treaties with the United States, resisted the 'removal' policy and was not defeated in its wars. Thus, it never legally signed away its land rights. The Court of Claims estimated the land to be worth $50 million, but Congress decided to pay only $12 million. All claims are based on land prices at the time they were stolen. The Seminoles have refused the payment, demanding their land. Their tribal leaders have compared the $12 million with the figure of $350 million given by the United States to anti-Castro Cubans."[18]

Hunting and Fishing Rights

Hunting and fishing rights were also guaranteed in the original treaties with the Indian nations. Nonetheless, Indians have been constantly prevented from exercising these rights. Hunting and fishing is not merely a form of recreation for Indians, it is their livelihood, since most of the reservations are extremely improverished. Indians have waged many legal battles in response to the curtailment of their rights. There have been many demonstrations, some of them resulting in violence.

The poor quality of both fish and other meat products sold on the reservations make it almost a necessity for Indians to be able to hunt and fish. The following cases are isolated examples of legal struggles for hunting and fishing rights for Indians.

"In a dispute over licensing, the Solicitor General ruled for the Bureau of Indian Affairs, in 1936, 'though hunting rights of the Minnesota Chippewa were not written into the treaties, they are still to be upheld by virtue of the larger rights possessed by them on land occupied and used'. The customary rights of a tribe remain inviolable unless specifically rescinded in treaties. Thus, the Red Lake Tribe of Chippewas was not required to purchase the licenses and migratory bird stamps in order to hunt docks, geese, etc."[19]

In another case, the federal government ruled in 1969 that the Indians throughout an eight-state region of the Southwest and the Rockies could not gather pinyon nuts unless they paid a tax. This harvest has been of economic importance to Indians for centuries, providing not only a major food source but a commercial base as well.

Self-Determination

Indian resistance has excelled in recent years. Self-determination and sovereignty is very important to them now; they are culturally and religiously different. Also, the great infringements on Indian sovereignty make them more determined than ever. The problems that the Indians have encountered with assimilation have been the complete failure of education programs for their people, culture genocide, continual rejection of Indian projects geared toward self-determination, violation of their rights. Until there is clear recognition of Indian sovereignty, rights and self-determination, there will always be Indian resistance.

The Sovereign Immunity of the Tribe

A key to being truly a sovereign entity is a nation's power to make itself exempt from a suit. Indian tribes do not have this power in and of itself; Congress may authorize suits against the tribes. In *United States* v. *United States Fidelity Company*,[20] the Supreme Court said: "These Indians are exempt from suit without Congressional authorization. It is as though the immunity which was theirs as sovereigns passed to the United States for their benefits, as their tribal properties did."[21] Indian tribes do have conditional immunity from suits.

Conclusion

This chapter has taken a broad look at some of the key areas associated with American Indian sovereignty. While the Indians are not internationally recognized as sovereign, they do possess some degree of sovereignty in the United States. This has been recognized in some court cases and in some legislation.

Overall, the Indians are not really recognized as a sovereign entity within the United States. There have been great infringements on Indian sovereignty throughout American history, whether by violence, federal and state infringements on Indian sovereignty, or violation of Indians's hunting and fishing rights, etc. With this, there has been continual Indian resistance to assimilation and violation of their rights.

"Largely through his own effort, the tribal Indian is no longer the forgotten American.[22] His efforts have raised the question whether his *sui generis* role in the federal system can or should survive. It has been said that 'to the extent the tribal Indian asserts an inherent right or tribal self-government, he has not truly mainfested his consent to be governed wholly under the internal government set forth in the Constitution'.[23] Many tribal Indians would heartily agree with this appraisal.[24] The Constitution was not designed with tribes in mind. Congress has been caught between changing tides of opinion running from full separation to total assimilation, but neither is immediately achievable. The reality is that the tribe cannot be separate, if only because historical forces and the Indian's already achieved partial integration are irreversible.[25] The effort must be to find some imaginative accommodation of tribal interests in cultural identity consistent with the federal system and the near certain assimilation of the tribe in the future."[26]

This chapter is not meant to be confused with the theme of the book. It is simply meant to give the reader a basic understanding of American Indian sovereignty in terms of United States recognition and Indian self-determination.

Chapter 10 will review the problem in jurisdicational allocation and some of the solutions that can be offered.

Footnotes
Chapter 9

1. e.g. Restatement of Foreign Relations Law of the United States, Sec. 4 (1965).

2. W. Friedman, O. Lissitzen & R. Pugh, *Cases and Materials of International Law* 180 (7th ed. 1972).

3. J. Starke, *An Introduction to Internaitonal Law* 180 (7th ed. 1972).

4. Id. at 181; Frederick Martone, "American Indian Tribal Self-Government in the Federal System: Inherent Right or Congressional License," *Notre Dame Lawyer,* Vol. 51, No. 4, Ap. 76, p. 603.

6. *Ibid.,* p. 604.

8. 25 U.S.C. Sections 1301–1341 (1976).

9. Bishin, "Judicial Review in Democratic Theory," 50 S. *California Law Review,* 1099, 1102 (1977).

10. Burnett, "An Historical Analysis of the 1968 Indian Civil Rights Act," 9 Horv. J. Legis. 557, 579 (1972).

13. 25 U.S.C. Sec. 1302 (1976); Alvin J. Ziontz, "After Martinez: Civil Rights Under Tribal Government," *UCD Law Review,* Vol. 12, No. 1, March, 1979, p. 2.

15. See *Report of the NAICJA Long Range Planning Project,* 37–40 (1978).

17. See American Indian Lawyer Training Program, Indian Self-Determination and the Rolf of Tribal Courts, 68 (1977).

18. William Meyer, *Native Americans: The New Indian Resistance,* International Publishers, New York, 1971, p. 65.

19. *Ibid.,* p. 68.

22. "The Indian: The Forgotten American," 81 *Har. L. Review,* 1818 (1968).

23. "Sovereignty, Citizenship and the Indian," 15 *Ariz. Law Review,* 973, 1001-1002 (1973).
24. "Henderson & Barsh, Oyate Kin Hoye Keyuga U Pe," *Harvard Law School Bulletin,* April, 1974 at 10, June, 1974 at 10, Fall, 1974 at 17.
25. See note, Supra note 294 at 1840.
26. Martone, p. 634.

Cases

Chapter 9

5. 20 A.M.J. International L. 574 (1926).
6. Id. at 577.
7. 436 U.S. 49 (1978).
11. *Talton* v. *Mayes,* 163 U.S. 376 (1896); *Navive American Church* v. *Navajo Tribal Council,* 272 F.2d 131 (10th Cir. 1959).
12. *Cherokee Nation* v. *Hitchcock,* 187 U.S. 294 (1902); *Lone Wolf* v. *Hitchcock,* 187 U.S. 294 (1902); *Talton* v. *Mayes,* 163 U.S. 376 (1896); *U.S.* v. *Kagama,* 118 U.S. 275 (1886).
16. *Halona* v. *MacDonald* reported in five Indian; L. Rep. Section m at 119 (1978).
20. 309 U.S. 506 (1940).
21. Id. at 512.

Chapter 10
Problems and Solutions in the Jurisdictional Scheme
in Indian Country

Two things have been determined throughout this book in terms of criminal jurisdiction on Indian land. One is that criminal jurisdiction is determined by a complex and inconsistent body of law which, more often than not, makes it incomprehensible to the people who live under it. The other is that the existing jurisdictional scheme has been responsible for erosion of tribal sovereignty, and has continued to impede the Indian effort toward self-determination.

The magnitude of this subject prevents identification of all the existing problems, and equally prevents the proposal of all possible solutions.

(1) One disadvantage of the three-fold jurisdictional system of federal, state and tribal governments—courts over criminal jurisdiction of Indian country—is the confusion and sometimes duplication of law enforcement efforts. The majority of problems in this area are those of definition. Application of the rules governing jurisdiction may prove to be difficult in cases where the race of the victim or the offender is not known, difficult in those cases when the status of the place of the crime as Indian land is unclear,[1] and difficult in multi-racial offenses.

There are basic jurisdictional problems in determining what is Indian country and who is an Indian. To be able to deal more effectively with these problems, Congress should eliminate some of the many definitions of an Indian to allow tribal courts a greater degree of territorial jurisdiction.[2] With respect to the fact that the tribe bears the burden of territorial violations, it should be empowered to prosecute such offenses without the difficulties of determining the race of the offender. The effect of this would be to clarity the bounds of federal and state jurisdiction as well.

"One solution to the problems which the definition of 'Indian country' poses is that in checkerboard areas, i.e., areas in which Indian land is interspersed with non-Indian land, the definition should reflect the predominant character of the land.[3] For example, land primarily occupied by Indians should be classified as Indian country for purposes of allocating criminal jurisdiction. Similarly, land occupied primarily by non-Indians should be excluded from the definition of Indian country. This proposal would increase the scope of tribal authority in non-reservation land inhabited by Indians with the desirable effect of encouraging Indian self-government and tribal institutions."[4]

(2) A second major criticism of the existing jurisdictional set-up deals with the impact of Public Law 280. There has been sharp criticism of the effect of Public Law 280 on Indian self-government by Indian leaders.[5] Some of these leaders have referred to those lands under state jurisdiction as lawless no man's land. The states not only have failed to assume the responsibilities of Public Law 280, but they have also impeded Indian's efforts toward tribal sovereignty.[6]

The result of the three-fold approach of Public Law 280 has been a lack of national uniformity in state-tribal relations. California has jurisdiction with respect to all reservations for both criminal and civil matters. On the other hand, Mississippi exercises no jurisdiction under Public Law 280, and thus all reservations in Mississippi are under federal jurisdiction.[7] More confusion is added by a provision which permits retrocession of any measure of jurisdiction to the federal government after once assumed by a state pursuant to Public Law 280.[8] Although this measure was to provide the means of returning jurisdiction to the Indians via the federal government, an insufficent amount of effort has been spent on plans to prepare the various tribes to use the retrocession provision to their advantage."[9]

(3) A major question that has not been answered is the extent to which Indian tribal courts may exercise criminal jurisdiction over non-Indians who commit offenses in violation of tribal law on Indian reservations. In *Ex Parte Kenyon*[10] in 1878, a circuit court held that the Cherokee Nation did not have jurisdiction over a non-Indian United States citizen residing in Kansas. The court ruled that the offender must be an Indian for the tribal court to have jurisdiction.[11]

"The Kenyon decision is regarded as having heavily damaged[12] Indian sovereignty. Kenyon is still relied upon as authority for denying tribal courts criminal jurisdiction over non-Indian offenders.[13] Several Indian tribes have recently challenged this holding and have, on their own initiative, assumed jurisdiction over non-Indians within their reservation.[14] The tribes have sought to justify this assumption of justifiction by enacting ordinances which stipulate that any person who enters the reservation by virtue of his entry impliedly consents to the jurisdiction of tribal courts."[15]

In a recent study of the American Indian and justice, the National American Indian Court Judges Association conducted several interviews with reservation Indians between July 1, 1972 and December 1, 1973.[16] The findings of these interviews indicate that many Indian leaders and law enforcement officials believe that Indian courts and policy must have jurisdiction over non-Indians. There is also a considerable amount of resentment on the part of the Indians concerning the double standard which results when non-Indians are not made subject to tribal laws. The situation is even more pronounced when an Indian is punished under tribal law for a misdemenaor and the Indian's non-Indian accomplice is set free. The effect of this is to engender in tribal members a mistrust of the law, resulting in frustration, hostility, and a feeling that the law is grossly unfair.[17]

"The implied consent ordinances are a desirable means to remedy some of the jurisdictional confusion. The Solicitor General of the Department of the Interior has challenged the legality of such ordinances.[18] Thus, the viability of this Indian-initiated remedy is hindered by the 1878 Kenyon ruling and the recent 1970 opinion of the Solicitor General. Opposition to implied consent ordinances is not justified. A state can legislate for its general welfare by the means of implied consent jurisdiction over non-residents.[19] Indian tribes, recognized as sovereign dependent nations,[20] should be allowed to promote tribal welfare by obtaining implied consent jurisdiction over non-Indians on reservations."[21]

(4) The funding for the administration of criminal justice in Indian country is very limited. The federal, state, and tribal governments experience problems in this area.

Things such as investigation difficulties, distances, and limited personnel for reservation caseloads hinder the federal government. Many Indians complain that those Indians who commit the most serious offenses either go unpunished altogether or only receive the misdemeanor sentences of the tribal courts.[22] State governments, more often than not fail to provide adequate enforcement services for reservations, mostly because those taxes that are normally available for law enforcement purposes cannot be collected in Indian country.[23] The tribe's own judicial systems, are ineffective because they lack the monetary and personnel resources necessary to properly operate them. Indian tribes vary in areas such as traditions and customs, the amount of land in the reservation, and their economic assets. Programs which would add to tribal resources resulting in more effective tribal courts are lacking at both the federal and state level.

"Federal policy in its reliance on state jurisdiction [where the state has assumed jurisdiction under Public Law 280] and federal jurisdiction ignores the tribal court's potential to function most effectively as the authority most directly involved with the affairs of the Indian reservation. A change in policy is suggested. Remedial action would require increased federal funding for tribal judicial systems and training programs for tribal personnel. These efforts would conceivably offer two benefits. First, by dealing directly with the needs of the tribal community, the administration of justice would be more effective. Second, this would encourage the tribes in their effort to promote internal sovereignty."[24]

Conclusion

This chapter has examined the complexity of the criminal jurisdiction allocation. It has looked at some of the criticisms of the present three-fold set-up as well as some suggestions and possible solutions for improvement of jurisdictional allocation of Indian country.

The complex system of criminal jurisdiction is a problem unique to those Native Americans residing in Indian country. Indians, as subjects of the tribal, state, and federal governments must deal with multiple and often conflicting assertions of authority. To alleviate the problems connected with the present division of criminal justice, several things would be required: (1) recognition of Indian self-determination and tribal integrity, (2) legislative and judicial attention, and (3) a balance of concession somewhere between the United States Government's role of power, control, and authority over the Indians and the Indian's continual attempt at self-government.

Footnotes

Chapter 10

2. National American Indian Court Judges Association, Justice and the American Indian, "Examination of the Basis of Tribal Law and Order Authority," Vo. IV, 9 (1974).

3. Id. at 26.

4. Immigration, Alienage and Nationality, "Criminal Jurisdiction in Indian Country," *UDC Law Review,* Vol. 8, 1975, p. 448.

5. Wendell Chino, President of the NCAI, President Johnson Presents Indian Message to Congress, 1 Indian Record 28 (March, 1968).

6. Id.

7. N.A.I.C.J.A., *Justice and the American Indian,* "The Impact of Public Law 280 Upon the Administration of Justice on Indian Reservations," Vol. 1, 88 (1974).

8. This provision was added by the 1968 Civil Rights Act and is codified at 25 U.S.C., Sec. 1323 (a) 1970.

9. See Goldberg, Supra note 105, at 558; "Criminal Jurisdiction in Indian Country," p. 448.

12. Basis of Tribal Law and Order, Supra note 5 at 32.

13. Id. at 39.

14. Id. note 5 at 50.

15. E.G., The Salt River Ordinance No. S.R.O. 11-72; Criminal Jurisdication in Indian Country, p. 450.

16. Basic of Tribal Law and Order, Supra note 5 at 8.

17. Id. at 52.

18. Basis of Tribal Law and Order, Supra note 5 at 39.

19. E.G., states have passed laws by which non-residents impliedly consent to the jurisdiction of the state with regard to service of process and intoxication tests for drivers.

21. Criminal Jurisdiction in Indian Country, p. 451.

22. D. Klein, Criminal Jurisdiction in Indian Country: The Policeman's Dilemma 1 (1973).

23. Comment, South Dakota Indian Jurisdiction, 11 *S.D. Law Review* 101, 115 (1966).

24. Criminal Jurisdiction in Indian Country, p. 458.

Cases

Chapter 10

1. *People* v. *Carmen* 36 C.2d 768, 228 p. 2d 281 (1951).
10. 14 F. Cas. 353 (no. 7720) (C.C.W.D. Ark. 1878).
11. 14 F. Cas. at 355.
20. 31 U.S. (6 Pet.) 515,561 (1832).

Chapter 11
Have the Indians been Treated Fairly?

The topic of historical perspective of the criminal jurisdictional set-up, and the resultant problems of Indian country has been very interesting. This chapter will offer a general analysis of the monograph and address the issue of whether the Indians have been treated fairly.

The Constitution

In reviewing the historical shaping of U.S.-Indian relations, let's take a look at the Constitutional section which is the real basis of United States-Indian interaction. Article I, Section 8, Clause 3 is the section of the Constitution which gives Congress the power to regulate commerce with the Indian tribes. The United States Government used this commerce clause as the means for all dealings with Indians, simply for lack of any other passages in the Constitution that mention Indians in any real sense. With the United States being a democratic nation, they probably wanted to make any and all moves within the limits of the Constitution. They, therefore, used that commerce clause as their justification for the poor way in which Indians were treated in the past and the way they continue to be treated. It is interesting to note that the Constitution, being the powerful document that it is, hardly mentions anything about the

111

Indians who had already occupied this territory. In *The Federalist Papers,* the few words mentioned in the book were negative toward the Indians. It is hard to imagine that great men held in such esteem such as Hamilton, Madison, and Jay could be willing to look at a fellow human being as a savage. With those shapers of the Constitution having the opinion that they had of the Indians and with American policy toward Indians based upon an interpretation of the little said about them in the Constitution, it is little wonder that the Indians have been humiliated, abused, and robbed of their homeland.

Defining the Indian

The varying definitions of the Indian, Indian country, and Indian title are broad, unclear, and sometimes overlapping. It is certainly important, in terms of criminal and civil jurisdiction, that there is a basis upon which an Indian can be determined. This is necessary for many reasons, including the determination of what court has jurisdiction, whether a crime is a misdemeanor or a felony, the amount of governmental financial assistance one is entitled to. However, in many cases, the federal, state, and even the tribal courts and governments, have a different definition of what an Indian is and what constitutes Indian country. This tends to be confusing not only for the different governments but also for Indians and non-Indians. In addition, many of the definitions used are devised and suited to the advantage of the particular government that established the definition. I feel that a universally accepted definition of an Indian and Indian country should be made applicable to all governments and their laws relating to Indian affairs. This would not only eliminate a lot of the confusion resultant from the current diverse definitions, but would also make the definitions of Indians, Indian country, and Indian title clear and singular so that they can apply to all Indians.

Early Legislation and Treaties

The early legislation and treaties between the Indians and the United States Government stem from a common base:

expansion. The various trade and intercourse acts were specific-ally designed by the federal government to limit state and individual dealings with Indians. At the same time, the federal government's intentions were to establish control of Indians. It seems that this was the government's early effort—to establish sovereignty over the Indians. With the federal government con-trolling the interest in Indians, it has allowed them to almost totally control all matters of importance concerning the Indians of the United States.

The treaties between the United States and the Indians were totally self-centered by the federal government. The govern-ment's efforts were strictly for expansion and did not really concern itself with the resultant plight of the Indians. Not only the federal government, but the state government, as well, accomplished much of their treaties with the Indians through trickery, deceit, forgery, and broken promises. Such unjust practices had a great effect on the United States Government-Indian relations. It gave the United States more land and expansion as the Indians either gave up their property through illegal treaties, force, unfair treaties, or bribery. This also led to many deaths of Indians due to disease, starvation, battle as they were forced to do things that were to their disadvantage. Much of the problem with the treaty-making has surfaced today with the Indians having problems with fishing and water rights, rightfully owned territory, taxes, and sovereignty.

Regardless of whether or not the Indian treaties were legal, they definitely were not fair and totally to the advantage of the United States. It was these treaties that really constituted the foundation of U.S.-Indian relations. With these treaties being unfair from the beginning, it constitutes an asterisk next to the United States remarkable progression in two hundred years.

The Legal Status of Indians

The government's Indian Removal Act and its partial recogni-tion of Indian sovereignty was again strictly an American government effort at expansion and sovereignty. With Andrew Jackson's State of the Union message outlining the Removal

Act, it was clear that the Act was strictly a legal means to allow the government to expand. In a sense, the Act was also for the protection of the Indians. Since the settlers were going to expand by force, if necessary, the Indian Removal Act allowed the Indians to move westward on their own. If they did so, they were allowed partial self-governance as long as it did not infringe with the United States laws or interests. The Removal Act did not really give the Indians a choice. They either moved westward voluntarily or stayed at the risk of losing their lives. This led to some fights and efforts by the Indians to keep their land. In the end, the Indians were virtually stripped of everything, reflected today by the poor living conditions on Indian reservations.

Criminal Jurisdiction in Indian Country

The allocation of criminal jurisdiction in Indian country is rather unclear, overlapping, and strictly to the advantage of the United States Government. The federal government has jurisdiction over the major crimes committed on Indian land. The state government has jurisdiction over some crimes within state boundaries and some of them have jurisdiction over major crimes through Public Law 280. The Indian government (courts) have very little criminal jurisdiction, even though Indian country is under its territory and certainly within its jurisdiction.

The writer's assessment of the criminal jurisdictional set-up is that it is unfair, biased, to the federal government's benefit, unclear, and inefficient. It is quite unfair and inefficient for several reasons: (1) The federal or state governments often will not send officials to investigate offenses on Indian territory because of the lack of concern, higher priority events, the time it takes to travel there, and monetary expenses that may be involved. The Indian courts, in these instances, cannot really do anything about these crimes because they do not have jurisdiction. (2) The Indian courts have no jurisdiction at all over non-Indians. Therefore, given the lack of the United States Government's concern over prompt attention to criminal matters on Indian land, it would not be very difficult for a non-Indian to use that to his advantage. (3) Indians who live on Indian land can also take advantage of the lack of real authority over major crimes on Indian land. (4) Given the minimum control that they have over major criminal conduct, the tribal officers tend to have little effect on criminal conduct on Indian land. This is also reflected in minor criminal conduct. (5) Though most Indian tribes have their own criminal codes for all criminal conduct on Indian land, they are really obsolete.

The tribal courts need to have more authority and power in criminal conduct and control of their conduct in Indian territory though they will never have complete control over all criminal conduct in Indian land. It is important that the tribal courts have more inupt in major criminal problems that occur on Indian land for better efficiency and effectiveness. In the present system, the tribal court authority is barely more than a figurehead. They have virtually no power unless the federal government gives it to them. The federal government does not bother to concern itself with minor criminal conduct and civil disputes. This is an insult to the Indians, because the government is telling them that they will control everything that is important with regard to their lives, but they can maintain their sovereignty on issues such as marriage. The present set-up of criminal jurisdictional allocation also holds true for civil jurisdiction. The same solutions for civil jurisdiction are necessary.

Indian Sovereignty

Indian sovereignty is basically unrealistic in terms of its definition. The Indians have no international recognition of sovereignty; the United States clearly has sovereignty of every area of major importance in United States territory concerning Indians. Any mention of Indian sovereignty is strictly a figurehead position or a degree of sovereignty granted to them by the United States Government. Once the United States acquired control of the territory through treaties, land ceding, trickery, the Indian Removal Act, etc., it has solidified its claim to sovereignty.

Even though the Indians claim such rights as hunting, fishing, and water, via early treaties, they are still fighting a losing battle. Some of the rights of Indians are protected, but it is because the United States wants to do so. It may be out of honor or out of a slight compassion. Nontheless, it has become quite apparent that the government decides and therefore treat the Indians in any way that they desire. This can be seen throughout the history of U.S.-Indian relations.

Analysis

The overall analysis of U.S.-Indian relations and criminal jurisdiction in Indian territory is that the system is totally unfair and geared toward the United States Government and its people. From the very beginning of U.S.-Indian relations (treaties, and Article I, Section 8 of the Constitution), it has been evident that the Indians were not thought of in the Constitution and the treaties were to the advantage of the United States Government. This has pretty much set the example for all U.S.-Indian relations since that time. The criminal jurisdictional allocation is clearly one-sided (geared toward the United States) and the tribal government has virtually no authority. The United States is the real sovereign power in this territory; the Indian has been constantly abused and taken advantage of.

Solutions

(1) The Indians should be allowed to maintain total sovereignty and maintenance of their culture (those that want to) as a test to see if they can accomplish it in an orderly fashion.

(2) All criminal jurisdiction in Indian territory should be under the jurisdiction of the tribal courts with an American school-trained set of officials or, perhaps, an American committee that could help administer and set up the court system.

(3) The Indians should be assimilated more into American society in terms of education, American methods, etc. and be allowed to use their increased knowledge to better administer their own culture.

(4) More of the original treaties between the federal government and Indians should be honored, without harrassment to allow the Indians some of the rights which they are entitled to such as fishing and water rights.

(5) There should be a continual effort on the part of the American government to achieve better relations and communication with the Indians.

Reflection

Reflecting on the Indian plight, there is no question in my mind that they have suffered greatly. The United States Government has taken advantage of and used the Indians for their own means. Though the Indian problems have been vast, they constitute another form of hardship that a race has had to suffer in the United States. Slavery and the resultant racism and prejudice accompanying it is another form of hardship evident in the United States today.

Conclusion

This book has examined the criminal jurisdiction set-up of Indian country and the problems associated with it. To do this, it has reviewed the definitions of Indians and Indian country, the Constitutional basis for United States-Indian interaction, important legislation regarding the shaping of the U.S.-Indian relations and jurisdiction, and the concept of Indian sovereignty. This has been accomplished with the use of research materials and by using cases that were either precedent-setting or clear examples of the subject matter.

Bibliography

1. State Government. Les Houston. *The States and Indian Jurisdiction,* 1977.

2. S. Lyman Tyler. *History of Indian Policy.* U.S. Department of Interior, BIA: Washington, D.C., 1973.

3. Lewis Mariam. *The Problem of Indian Administration.* John Hopkins Press, Maryland, 1928.

4. U.S. Code Annotated — *Title 18, Crimes and Criminal Procedure,* No. 1-370, 1081-1690, and 3001-3530. West Publishing Company, St. Paul, Minnesota, 1969.

5. *Laws of the United States Relating to Indian Affairs.* Washington, Government Printing Office, 1884.

6. Theodore W. Taylor. *The States and Their Indian Citizens.* U.S. Department of the Interior, BIA, Washington, D.C. 1972.

7. *Native American Rights Funds.* National Indian Law Library, Vol. 2, No. 1, Jan - Feb., 1973.

8. N.A.S.C. Land and Resources Edition. *Sovereignty Can't Be Legislated.* Vol. 3, No. 1, March, 1978.

9. Immigration, Alienage and Nationality. *The Allocation of Criminal Jurisdiction in Indian Country—Federal, State, and Tribal Relationships.* University of California, Davis Law Review, Vol. 8, 1975.

10. D. Klein, *Criminal Jurisdiction in Indian Country: The Policeman's Dilemma,* 1973.

11. National American Indian Court Judges Association, Justice and the American Indian, *Examination of the Basis of Tribal Law and Order Authority,* Vol. IV, 9, 1974.

12. William T. Hagan. *Indian Police and Judges.* Yale University Press, New Haven, 1966.

13.   League of Women Voters of Minnesota. *Indians in Minnesota.* St. Paul, Minnesota, 1971.

14.   Kirk Kickingbird and Karen Ducheneauz. *One Hundred Million Acres.* MacMillan Publishing Company, Incorporated, New York, 1973.

15.   Kenneth S. Murchison. *Decisions Relating to Indian Affairs.* Government Printing Office, Washington, 1973.

16.   William Meyer. *Native Americans: The New Indian Resistance.* International Publishers, New York, 1971.

17.   American Criminal Law Review. *"In Our Image. . .After Our Likeness": The Drive for the Assimilation of Indian Court Systems* by Kirk Kickingbird, Sp. 76, Vol. 13, New York.

18.   American Indian Treaties Publication. *Public Law 280: State Jurisdiction Over Reservation Indians.* Carole E. Goldberg. University of California, Series No. 1, 1975.

19.   Monroe E. Price. *Law and the American Indian.* The Bobbs-Merrill Company, Incorporated, Indianapolis, 1973.

20.   Robert E. Shaw, *Andrew Jackson: 1767–1845,* Oceana Publications, Incorporated, New York, 1969.

21.   *The Federalist Papers.* Alexander Hamilton, James Madison, and John Jay, A Mentor Book, New York, 1961.

22.   Alvin J. Ziontz. *After Martinez: Indian Civil Rights Under Tribal Government.* UDC Law Review, Vol. 12, No. 1, March 1979.

23.   Lawrence Rosen. *American Indians and the Law.* Transaction Books, New Jersey, 1976.

24.   Fred A. Seaton and Elmer F. Bennett. *Federal Indian Law,* U.S. Government Printing Office, Washington, 1958.

25.   Federick J. Martone. *American Indian Tribal Self-Government in the Federal System: Inherent Right or Congressional License?* Notre Dame Lawyer, Vol. 51, No. 4, Ap. 76.

References made to the following:

1.   U.S. Constitution.

2.   J. Starke. *An Introduction to International Law 180* (7th ed. 1972).

3.   F. Cohen. Handbook of Federal Indian Law, 1971.

4.   *The Indian Bill of Rights and the Constitutional Status of Tribal Governments.* 83 Harvard Law Review, 1969.

5.   Dowling, Criminal Jurisdiction Over Indians and Post-Conviction Remedies, 22 Montana Law Review, 165, 1961.

Index